**Managing Universities and Colleges:
Guides to Good Practice**

Series editors:

David Warner, Principal and Chief Executive, Swansea
Institute of Higher Education

David Palfreyman, Bursar and Fellow, New College, Oxford

This series has been commissioned in order to provide systematic
analysis of the major areas of the management of colleges and
universities, emphasizing good practice.

Current titles:
Allan Bolton: *Managing the Academic Unit*
Ann Edworthy: *Managing Stress*
Judith Elkin and Derek Law (eds): *Managing Information*
John M. Gledhill: *Managing Students*
Christine Humfrey: *Managing International Students*
Colleen Liston: *Managing Quality and Standards*
David Watson: *Managing Strategy*

Forthcoming titles include:
Andrew Paine: *Managing Hospitality Services*
Harold Thomas: *Managing Financial Resources*

MANAGING STRESS

Ann Edworthy

Open University Press
Buckingham · Philadelphia

Open University Press
Celtic Court
22 Ballmoor
Buckingham
MK18 1XW

email: enquiries@openup.co.uk
world wide web: www.openup.co.uk

and
325 Chestnut Street
Philadelphia, PA 19106, USA

First Published 2000

A catalogue record of this book is available from the British Library

ISBN   0 335 20405 8 (pb)   0 335 20406 6 (hb)

Library of Congress Cataloging-in-Publication Data
Edworthy, Ann, 1952–
    Managing stress / Ann Edworthy.
        p.   cm. – (Managing universities and colleges)
    Includes bibliographical references and index.
    ISBN 0–335–20406–6 – ISBN 0–335–20405–8 (pbk.)
    1. College teachers – Job stress—Great Britain.   2. Stress management
– Great Britain.   I. Title.   II. Series.
LB2333.3.E39   2000
155.9′042′02437–dc21   00–022496

Typeset by Graphicraft Limited, Hong Kong
Printed in Great Britain by The Cromwell Press, Trowbridge

CONTENTS

SERIES EDITORS'
INTRODUCTION

Post-secondary educational institutions can be viewed from a variety of different perspectives. For most of the students and staff who work in them they are centres of learning and teaching in which the participants are there by choice and consequently, by and large, work very hard. Research has always been important in some higher education institutions, but in recent years this emphasis has grown, and what for many was a great pleasure and, indeed, a treat, is becoming more of a threat and an insatiable performance indicator, which just has to be met. Maintaining the correct balance between quality research and learning/teaching, while the unit of resource continues to decline inexorably, is one of the key issues facing us all. Educational institutions as work places must be positive and not negative environments.

From another aspect, post-secondary educational institutions are clearly communities, functioning to all intents and purposes like small towns and internally requiring and providing a similar range of services, while also having very specialist needs. From yet another, they are seen as external suppliers of services to industry, commerce and the professions. These 'customers' receive, *inter alia*: a continuing flow of well qualified, fresh graduates with transferable skills; part-time and short course study opportunities through which to develop existing employees; consultancy services to solve problems and help expand business; and research and development support to create new breakthroughs.

However, educational institutions are also significant businesses in their own right. One recent study of the economic impact of higher education in Wales shows that it is of similar importance in employment terms to the steel or banking/finance sectors. Put another way,

Welsh higher education institutions (HEIs) spend half a billion pounds annually and create more than 23,000 full-time equivalent jobs. And it must be remembered that there are only 13 HEIs in Wales, compared with 171 in the whole of the UK, and that these Welsh institutions are, on average, relatively small. In addition, it has recently been realized that higher education in the UK is a major export industry with the added benefit of long-term financial and political returns. If the UK further education sector is also added to this equation, the economic impact of post-secondary education is of truly startling proportions.

Whatever perspective you take, it is obvious that educational institutions require managing and, consequently, this series has been produced to facilitate that end. The editors have striven to identify authors who are distinguished practitioners in their own right and, indeed, can also write. The authors have been given the challenge of producing essentially practical handbooks that combine appropriate theory and contextual material with many examples of good practice and guidance.

The topics chosen are of key importance to educational management and stand at the forefront of current debate. Some of these topics have never been covered in depth before and all of them are equally applicable to further as well as higher education. The editors are firmly of the belief that the UK distinction between these sectors will continue to blur and will be replaced, as in many other countries, by a continuum where the management issues are entirely common.

For well over a decade, both of the editors have been involved with a management development programme for senior staff from HEIs throughout the world. Every year the participants quickly learn that we share the same problems and that similar solutions are normally applicable. Political and cultural differences may on occasion be important, but are often no more than an overlying veneer. Hence, this series will be of considerable relevance and value to post-secondary educational managers in many countries.

Stress is a phenomenon that has always been with us, but during the past decade or so it seems to be developing into plague proportions. Certain recent landmark legal cases have raised the stakes for managers and could be key factors in explaining why their personal stress levels have risen so rapidly. But why should there be so many problems with stress in further and higher education? What is it about teaching and research or the nature of teachers and researchers that seems to make them so susceptible to stress?

In this important book Ann Edworthy deals with the issues of stress, step-by-step. She guides the reader to understand the negative and positive aspects of stress together with its manifestations. Ann then identifies the key sources of stress at work, before focusing on the precise stress factors in further and higher education. In the final chapters she deals with the health aspects of stress and approach towards its management. Throughout, Dr Edworthy uses practical examples and includes a number of self-test questionnaires. This book will therefore be of value not only to each of us as individuals, but in particular to those with responsibilities for managing others. The early identification of 'bad stress' is essential to ensure its mitigation and thereby avoid the human misery involved for everyone.

David Warner
David Palfreyman

ACKNOWLEDGEMENTS

I am indebted to many people for their support during the preparation of this book but there are individuals who deserve special acknowledgement. I would like to thank my father for his unending support and understanding when my patience was in short supply, John for his stylistic advice and encouragement and the many friends and colleagues who have contributed in different ways. I am grateful to Professor David Warner for having sufficient confidence in me to commission this book and to Peugeot for sponsoring my research, as without their assistance, much of my work on stress would not have been possible.

1

SETTING THE SCENE

What is stress?

In the past 10 to 20 years we have seen a major increase in the amount of press coverage on 'stress'. However, many would argue, particularly those who fought in World War II, that stress levels are no higher now than they were in the period 1939–45 and the media are exaggerating the facts. Perhaps the situation is appropriately explained by Newton *et al.* (1995). They suggest that as the term is more commonly used and understood, there will inevitably be an increase in the number of people who can identify their experiences as stress-related.

Although the term is used liberally, it is unlikely that any two people stating that they are 'stressed' are actually experiencing the same feelings. The concept of stress is quite elusive. It can be likened to the concepts of intelligence and happiness: everyone understands what we mean by the terms but each individual defines them differently. Some, for example, will say they are stressed when they are rushing to undertake scores of tasks in a limited time period. Others, however, are referring to the fact that their situation is such that it is causing their health to suffer.

The results of a survey reported by Hall (1994) showed that the employees now consider stress to be 'part and parcel' of the job. Of those surveyed:

- 70 per cent stated that stress was inevitable in their organization;
- 40 per cent indicated that their organization did not accept or recognize 'stress' as an illness;
- 58 per cent said that anyone who claimed to be 'stressed' at work would adversely affect their promotion prospects; and

- 74 per cent predicted that occupational stress would increasingly become more of an issue in the next five years.

Such findings are a real cause for concern. No worker should feel or be made to feel that high stress levels are the price that has to be paid if they wish to remain in employment.

In the UK the 1980s were characterized by industrial restructuring, which became a feature of the service sector in the early 1990s. In more recent years it has percolated into the public sector and civil service, where, according to Lazenby (1989: 3), 'Expectations of more from less, to a higher quality, and at a cheaper price are common to both producers and consumers alike'.

Education establishments, as well as other large organizations, function in an increasingly competitive environment that requires lecturers to respond to external challenges and pressures at a time when there are fewer resources available to them. At the same time, however, there are great expectations of them.

According to Hills (in Fisher 1994: ix) a lecturer now:

> has to teach increasingly more from a shrinking resource base and in the face of an explosion of knowledge and skills not seen before. The effort of having to research, administer and teach has become considerable, and, to many, unacceptable . . . Most academics will be the first to say their lives have become stressful.

Although the role of the lecturer is not traditionally considered by society to be one that elicits high levels of occupational stress, the situation has now changed. During the past 20 years or so, academics have witnessed some real changes in their work environment. Academic retrenchment has resulted in increased workloads, and a decrease in the level of control that lecturers have over their work (Melandez and Guzman 1983). This loss of autonomy has helped to provide the potential for the manifestation of high levels of work stress (Hickcox 1983).

High stress levels can have serious implications for the efficient functioning of a college. Increased absence through sickness and a high staff turnover are the usual outcomes of stress problems and these, in turn, can create new problems, such as stress among staff who are trying to cover for absent colleagues and stress among staff who have to make up for the reduced efficiency of stress-impaired colleagues.

Nevertheless, there continues to be a reluctance to admit to suffering from stress and this is generally attributed to a fear that it will be taken as a sign of weakness and incompetence. There is also the fear of the impact of such an admission upon the individual's career. This is evidenced by the fact that although some organizations provide stress counselling, it is often the case that individuals pay privately for their treatment and seek help outside the place of employment. This culture must be changed if the impact of stress is to be alleviated. In his opening speech at the TUC conference 'Stress: Who is Liable?', Frank Davies, Chairman of the Health and Safety Commission (HSC) said:

> People can be too frightened to admit that they are under stress, perhaps because they associate it within the stigma of mental illness or because people see it as a sign of some kind of weakness, and some organisations seem to be taking the view that stress is not their problem but an individuals.
>
> (Davies 1997: 3)

Cartwright and Cooper (1997) predict that as we go into the next millennium the incidence of stress is likely to increase. However, providing employees are educated to recognize the symptoms of stress, they will be in control of the situation and can act to prevent the stress manifesting itself. Once an individual knows what is wrong, and why, they can be taught how to change things for the better. After all, if you want to learn to play a musical instrument, or to improve your game of squash, you can arrange to have lessons. Similarly, if you want to manage and cope with stress and generally improve the quality of your life, you can seek advice.

In the following chapters I aim to familiarize the reader with the concept of stress. In particular, I discuss ways in which you can detect stress in yourself and others, factors responsible for stress and, perhaps most importantly, give advice on ways of developing coping mechanisms.

Approaches to stress

There are four main approaches to stress, which are discussed briefly in order to provide a background to the processes involved.

The physiological approach – what happens to the person

Selye (1974) was the first person to give credence to the concept of stress. He maintained that 'stress is not merely nervous tension' (p. 30) but is 'the non-specific response of the body to any demand

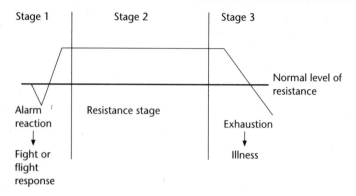

Figure 1.1 Sequence of events in a stressed reaction, based on the General Adaptation Syndrome

made upon it' (p. 27). His approach is based on the assumption that when under stress an individual will exhibit a triphasic response termed the General Adaptation Syndrome (GAS).

Selye (1956) described a model for prolonged stress in terms of physiological reactions. Stress from any source will trigger off the following sequence of events (Fig. 1.1).

1 The alarm reaction is the first response made by the body. It occurs when an individual perceives oneself to be in a threatening situation. Their body adapts to bring about the *fight or flight* response. There is a release of adrenaline, which mobilizes sugars, providing the energy to fight or run faster (flight), and reduces the supply of blood to non-essential parts of the anatomy. This ensures that energy is not wasted and means there can be an increase in the blood supply to essential organs.

2 The second stage is that of resistance. The production of chemicals in the body is maintained at a lower level as the body becomes used to the stressor.

3 The final stage of exhaustion occurs when the body's resources are eventually depleted. The adrenal glands do not function properly and this leads to a drop in blood sugar levels. This in turn leads to various psychosomatic disorders such as high blood pressure, heart disease, asthma and ulcers, and unless the pressure is removed it will ultimately lead to death.

The physiological response is not necessarily a very beneficial reaction to the stresses of modern life such as those produced from sitting trapped in a traffic jam or queuing in a supermarket, and it has been suggested (Dobson 1982) that this stereotyped physiological response to stress, which has become established in our genetic make-up, is a maladaption. The stresses we suffer today tend not to be short, sharp, dangerous encounters that require us to 'fight' or 'take flight', but are instead frustration and tensions of careers and family life, loud noise and crowds. In these changed circumstances our physiological response may actually do us harm.

The engineering approach (stimulus based approach)

This approach has gained its name because engineers use the word 'stress' for environmental forces acting upon a body. 'Stress' has been used in this sense by psychologists such as Cox (1990) and Fletcher (1988) who perceive occupational stress to be the result of pressure placed on an individual by negative environmental factors such as work overload, role conflict and poor working conditions. The engineering model is seen to parallel Hooke's Law of Elasticity, which relates 'stress' and 'strain'. Hooke's Law states that if the strain produced by a given element of stress falls within the 'elastic limit' of the material, the material will return to its original condition when the element of stress is removed. Should the strain pass beyond the elastic limit of the material some permanent damage is likely to result. Hence, if we assume that just as metals have different constituent properties and thus different elastic limits, so individuals have different levels of resistance to elements of stress. If the level of strain goes beyond the individual's tolerance level, permanent physiological or psychological damage is likely to occur.

The psychological approach

This approach is based on the interaction of the *person* and the *environment*. This approach focuses on the response pattern displayed by an individual, but it does, however, conceptualize stress as something that occurs within the individual when they are faced with demands that tax or exceed their resources. Perceptual and cognitive characteristics are thus considered vital in determining individual response differences to stress.

Some overlap exists between this approach and the engineering approach. The psychological approach, however, sees interaction occurring between the external demands, and the individual's constitutional vulnerability and defence mechanisms. Lazarus (1966, 1971) draws attention to the importance of the individual's ability to appraise the situation. Appraisal plays an important role in the psychological approach.

Cognitive science is concerned with the ways in which we think, know, apply logic and make decisions and, as such, plays an important part in the stress process. It is, after all, the cognitive processes that determine whether an individual views a situation as being stressful. An individual gathers experience throughout life, and then uses the information stored in the memory to predict outcomes of situations. Depending on the personality types, some people will view most events, even some traumatic ones, as positive, while others will always adopt a negative stance. According to Bandura (1977: 193), 'expectations of personal mastery affect both initiation and persistence of coping behaviour. The strength of people's convictions in their own effectiveness is likely to affect whether they will even try to cope with given situations'.

Low estimations of self-efficacy would lead lecturers to believe that they could not cope with the problem and would therefore be stressed. If lecturers believe in their ability to deal with everyday problems at work, they are more likely to perceive the situation as insignificant. Research shows that a person's self-efficacy will increase with coping successes (Butler 1988).

The transactional approach

This model represents an eclectic approach in that it draws from both the response and the stimulus based definitions; while simultaneously emphasizing the ecological and transactional nature of stress. It views stress as an individual perceptual phenomenon and suggests that this phenomenon arises when there is an imbalance between demand as estimated by the individual and their perceived ability to cope with that demand. This imbalance gives rise to the experience of stress, and then to a stress response. Coping strategies or responses aimed at alleviating stress are both psychological and physiological. Should the coping strategies prove ineffective, the stress may be prolonged and result in functional and/or structural damages. Cox and MacKay (1979) outline five recognizable stages in their transactional model.

1 The first stage is represented by the demands being made on the individual.
2 The second stage concerns the individual's perceptions of the demands. (Recall that stress is said to occur when there is an imbalance between the perceived demand and the individual's perception of their ability to meet that demand.)
3 The responses an individual makes to overcome stress are seen as the third stage of the model. The coping responses include cognitive

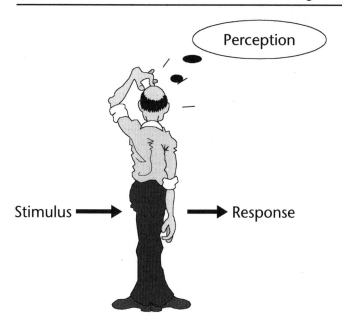

Figure 1.2 The stress cycle

strategies aimed at reducing the experience of stress by altering perceptual and cognitive function; for example, re-appraising the consequences of failure to meet external demand.
4 The fourth stage concerns the consequences of the coping responses. Here, both actual and perceived consequences are seen as important.
5 Feedback is the final stage. This occurs throughout, and is effective in shaping the outcome at each stage.

Possibly the transactional approach is the most readily applicable to everyday life as it is the only approach to contain the feedback element.

Although many different views of stress have been proposed, there appears to be a consensus that stress is a process that can occur when there is an unresolved mismatch between the perceived pressures of the situation and the individual's ability to cope (Fig. 1.2).

Good stress versus bad stress

It is important to remember that not all stress is inherently bad or destructive. 'Eu-stress' is the term used to describe the level of stress

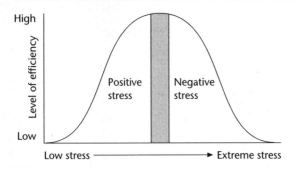

Figure 1.3 The relationship between stress and performance

that is good for you and is one of a person's best assets for achieving peak performance and managing minor crises. It does, however, have the potential for turning into 'distress', and it is this latter manifestation of stress that causes our body wear and tear. It can be compared to a car that is being revved up but not moving forward.

By definition, work should be demanding and, at times, place individuals under pressure. It is the demanding and challenging aspects of work that elicit improved performance from workers, and consequently enhance their self-esteem and job satisfaction. However, although some stress is a natural characteristic in our domestic and work lives, distress is not. Managers therefore have to promote the level of stress that leads to achievement while avoiding the detrimental effects of stress to reach unacceptable levels.

Yerkes and Dodson (1908) examined the relationship between stress and performance. Initially a person's performance increases under pressure until an optimum level has been reached. From here, performance begins to decline if more pressure is brought to bear, and, if the pressure is not reduced, performance is impaired and the individual's health may suffer. The way in which stress levels can be optimized will depend on whether the stress is short or long term in nature. Short-term stress occurs in situations that are confrontational, sporting events, visiting the dentist, giving a speech, and so on, and optimizing stress involves the short-term management of adrenaline to maximize performance. In the long term, where adrenaline has been released over long periods, optimizing stress focuses on the management of health and energy.

As Figure 1.3 shows, when your stress levels are too high, your performance is affected due to the physiological and psychological effects of the stress: poor health, tiredness and exhaustion. If, however, you are not under any real pressure, you will lack motivation and,

Questionnaire 1: Are you in the right job?

	Yes	No
1 Did you always want to be a lecturer?	☐	☐
2 Have you enjoyed, and are you enjoying your career?	☐	☐
3 Would you choose the same career if you could turn the clock back?	☐	☐
4 Does your work make full use of your abilities and have the appropriate level of responsibility?	☐	☐
5 Do you have the opportunity to develop yourself?	☐	☐
6 Do you look forward to going into college?	☐	☐
7 Do you get along with your senior colleagues?	☐	☐
8 Do you get along with your peer group?	☐	☐
9 Would you be happy to remain in the same organization for another ten years?	☐	☐
10 Do you feel that the organization cares about its staff?	☐	☐
11 Are you satisfied with your salary?	☐	☐
12 Do you feel staff are treated fairly and equitably?	☐	☐
13 Do you go home most days feeling that you achieved something?	☐	☐
14 Do you enjoy trying to motivate students?	☐	☐
15 Do you enjoy trying to help students attain their potential?	☐	☐
16 Are you satisfied with your promotional prospects?	☐	☐

Now add up the number of 'Yes' answers and the number of 'No' answers.
If you have over 11 'Yes' answers, you are generally happy with your job.

A score of 6–11 indicates that elements of your work are causing you real concern. These need to be looked at closely and action should be taken to overcome the problems. One way of doing this might be to arrange an appraisal interview with your head of department or line manager to discuss these issues.

A score of 0–6 shows there is definite incompatibility between yourself and your job. Is it the wrong job for you or maybe the wrong organization? You need to give serious thought to this, reassess your situation and take the necessary remedial action.

(Adapted from Stewart 1998)

again, your performance will be impaired. The ideal situation is to maintain your stress levels in the middle, shaded area. Here, you will experience a level of pressure or stress that will motivate without over-stressing and you will be able to function efficiently and effectively.

If you are in the 'wrong' job, your level of stress will be high. You cannot expect to change the system but if the job makes you unhappy you can change to a more appropriate type of employment. The questionnaire for lecturers is intended only as a guide to your person/job fit (Questionnaire 1). It should, however, indicate any major problems; if there are any, you need to give careful thought to your future.

Stress, the individual and work

Stress can result in physical and mental ill health, a lowering of job satisfaction and a loss of sense of achievement. These changes, by their very nature, will impair the quality of that individual's life (see Fig. 1.4).

Figure 1.4   Effects of stress on the individual

Long-term exposure to stress may also impact on family relation-ships and can result in marital breakdown and the social isolation of the person concerned. As a stress counsellor I frequently meet individuals who are experiencing high stress levels at work and, as a result, return home in an antisocial mood. This often leads to friction in their relationship with their partner, which, in turn, means the following day gets off to a bad start. Regrettably, the damage to the relationship can be irretrievable before the individual seeks help to overcome the problems at work, and separations or divorces are common.

A healthy work environment is one where:

- levels of stress are low;
- organizational commitment and job satisfaction are high;
- absenteeism and turnover rates are low;
- individual relationships are good;
- fear of litigation is absent;
- safety and accident records are good.

Unfortunately, most, if not all UK organizations could improve on most of these criteria, and this indicates the presence of high stress levels.

The Department of Health estimates that 80 million working days are lost every year due to stress related illnesses and they further suggest that up to 25 per cent of the British workforce is affected by the problem. Stressed workers do not think clearly and have difficulty concentrating. Job performance will, therefore, be impaired. Research shows that 60–80 per cent of accidents at work are stress related. It is thus evident that high levels of occupational stress create a burden for the employee, the employer and society, the last being affected through the costs incurred to cover health and social security payments.

2

MANIFESTATIONS OF STRESS

Before we can begin to look at the methods that can be implemented to reduce stress, we need to be able to recognize the signs of stress in ourselves and others.

Stages of stress

The body will respond to any situation in order to achieve its top physical condition to cope with what is happening. To begin with, the physiological reaction will be the same, regardless of whether the event is pleasant or threatening, happy or depressing, thrilling or perilous. The 'stress hormones' released by the body enable the individual to perform feats far beyond its normal capacity; for example in traffic accidents it has been known for one person to lift a vehicle to free someone who has been trapped.

During this initial stage of stress, the individual behaves as if they have an over-active thyroid. Tasks are undertaken faster than usual. They will eat faster but probably feel that they cannot afford to take a lunch break and will therefore be more inclined to snack on a packet of crisps or a bar of chocolate. Throughout the day this person may make many cups of tea or coffee but will rarely find time to drink any. Over a short period of time this amount of stress is not harmful and indeed acts as a motivator. After a while, however, tiredness will be experienced and may be accompanied by feelings of anxiety and frustration. The quality of work produced will suffer. Stage 2 has been entered.

During Stage 2, the person will feel as if they are being 'driven', and tiredness and fatigue are permanent features. Ironically, this is

Table 2.1   The stages of stress

Stage 1	Mobilizing energy 'Fight or flight'	Short term	An example might be meeting a deadline such as marking 300 exam scripts in 48 hours.
Stage 2	Consuming energy	Long term	An example might be having to spend 4–6 hours every evening preparing lectures for a new course. There is a feeling of 'there is no escape'.
Stage 3	Draining energy	Illness	There is a definite feeling of suffering from stress and inability to keep up the pace. The result might be illness and possibly death.

often the time when the person experiences great difficulty in getting to sleep, and even when they go to sleep, they wake up even earlier than before. This may lead to indulgence in 'comfort' substance such as chocolate, spicy food, alcohol or cigarettes. Because energy is being expended in an attempt to sustain the pace, the fatigue could result in memory deficiency.

Over a sustained period of time such levels of stress will damage the person's health. Stomach upsets, headaches and migraines are some of the more common symptoms, and the effects of stress on the nervous system may cause cramps and leg twitching, particularly at night. As this high level of stress continues the person may begin to feel a sense of failure and become ill more frequently. Employees often start to feel exploited by management and morale and job satisfaction begin to plummet. Eventually, there is a depletion of the body's resources and Stage 3 is entered. Everyone moves between the stages at different speeds and under different situations but we all have the potential to reach Stage 3, which ultimately results in death if the stress cannot be managed. The stress stages are summarized in Table 2.1.

Some stress can be mentally stimulating but too much pressure affects our thought processes and our thinking may become muddled and irrational. It becomes much more difficult to make decisions and the time is often spent on negative thoughts and worrying about everything. In simple terms, the mind becomes tired, the individual has difficulty concentrating and the memory becomes unreliable. The main effects of high stress levels on the intellectual function are:

- frequently having a thick cotton wool head (even without excessive alcohol);
- loss of former high concentration;
- loss of former reliable memory;
- a new inability to reach satisfactory decisions;
- new difficulty in dismissing problems from the mind; and
- insomnia.

All are evidence of a tired mind.

During Stage 3 stress, the energy drain has a detrimental effect on physical health. The most common ways in which the stress manifests are:

- difficulty breathing;
- recurrent headaches;
- ringing in the ears or frequent head noises;
- frequent use of antacids or other self-prescribed drugs;
- vomiting and nausea;
- palpitations and chest pain;
- frequent heartburn, stomach cramps, diarrhoea, and inability to swallow;
- sleep disturbances;
- trembling under any extra pressure, leg cramps or pain, and twitching in limbs;
- cardiac and rhythm disturbances;
- feeling that you may pass out;
- getting any illness that is around;
- profuse sweating.

All are evidence of failing physical health.

It is important to note that there are bodily changes that may be present but of which the sufferer may not actually be aware. They can be serious and in some cases life threatening, and it is crucial that anyone under Stage 3 stress seeks medical attention. These bodily changes include:

- increased blood pressure and heart rate;
- blood shunting (diversion of the flow) to muscles;
- increased blood glucose level;
- increased adrenaline production by adrenal gland;
- reduced gastrointestinal peristalsis; and
- pupillary dilation.

Emotional health will also be affected and the individual concerned will appear to have a 'changed' personality. The predominant emotions exhibited are anger and irritation and the person is likely to overreact to situations. Signs of energy drain in emotional health include:

- fear;
- a feeling of being very low and dulled;
- panic reactions;
- anger;
- denial;
- all joy, laughter and pleasure have dried up;
- tears seem frequently very near for no reason;
- withdrawal; and
- inappropriate emotions.

All are evidence of exhausted emotional health.

Chronic exposure to high levels of work stress may further lead to the destruction of the human spirit. This condition is known as 'burnout' and, like stress, it has serious effects on work performance and health. The problem is particularly prevalent in occupations that involve responsibility for others, such as lecturing.

Burnout, according to Maslach and Jackson (1984) can be measured in terms of three elements: emotional exhaustion, depersonalization and perceived inadequacy. In lecturing, the emotional exhaustion can result from continually striving to help students to succeed and to achieve the grades they need to follow their chosen careers. Depersonalization may be the result of lecturers seeing students as objects and having little interest in each individual. They would merely deliver their lectures at the appropriate times and have little or no concern for their students' progress or welfare. In situations where lecturers felt that their efforts were not producing the desired results their levels of job satisfaction would be low and feelings of inadequacy could result.

Signs of stress at work

Most of us accept and understand that anything mechanical needs to be looked after and serviced regularly in order to keep it in good working order. Indeed, we also look out for tell-tale signs that something is wrong, as this will enable us to deal with it at an early stage, thus avoiding, perhaps, more serious damage. It seems illogical, therefore, that many people are not aware of the signs to look for to ascertain if they are functioning properly or whether they are experiencing stress and all its manifestations.

The signs and symptoms of each stage of stress have been discussed but let us now look at the signs of stress at work. Quite often it may appear that a once motivated colleague is no longer committed to the job and their total lack of interest can be perceived as inefficiency. Such behavioural changes may be the result of the manifestations of high stress levels.

The following are some of the signs of stress at work. It may be possible to detect one or more of them in yourself or others. If highly stressed an individual may:

- *Disregard high priority tasks* Lecturers are continually faced with numerous administrative tasks as well as the everyday duties involved in lecturing. An inability to think rationally may result in lower priority tasks being completed first, which can lead to ill feeling among all parties concerned.
- *Reduce the time given to each task* Colleagues who have proved themselves capable of delivering high quality courses, documents and so on may submit work of a poorer standard.
- *Re-define boundaries to shift responsibility* People who have always cooperated and functioned as team members may begin to refuse to accept responsibility and develop a 'nothing to do with me' attitude.
- *Block out new information* This person will show no interest in learning new skills or show any willingness to change practices and procedures.
- *Involve themselves only superficially* The lecturer's record of absenteeism may not change but they will go into college, deliver their lectures, tutorials, and whatever other duties are mandatory and not partake in any optional meetings. Comments such as 'Just give me my timetable and I will teach it' are common and the person shows no interest in course developmental work or similar activities.
- *Display inappropriate humour* The lecturer may laugh at quite serious issues being discussed or will burst out laughing, for no apparent reason, during a lull in conversation.
- *Give up easily* As soon as a problem is encountered, such as computer failure, they will abandon the task in hand. No consideration would be given to obtaining technical support.
- *Develop 'paralysis by analysis'* Whenever asked to undertake a task they will needlessly ask 'Why?', 'How?', 'Where?' or 'What is the point?', and make statements such as 'It won't work' or 'This is a waste of time'.
- *Develop memory loss* The person may forget what they wished to relate in mid-sentence.

Behavioural changes of a more general nature may also indicate extreme stress. If these are detected in a colleague it is best to report the matter to a more senior colleague who would be in a position to provide the services of a trained counsellor. Although we all wish to help and support our colleagues it is very important to get expert help as an untrained person may unwittingly do more harm than good. These behavioural changes may include:

- an increase in particular personality traits
  - a person who is naturally tidy will become excessively so
  - a person who is normally critical will become a real trial to work with
  - a person who is quick-tempered will become even more so;
- changes in eating habits
  - a 'greedy' person will eat even more
  - a person with little interest in food will eat even less;
- crying spells, where the person isn't sure why they are so upset;
- excessive silence;
- increased alcohol consumption;
- increased smoking; and
- withdrawal.

The particular signs and symptoms exhibited will vary from person to person.

Personality types and stress

As we have already seen, it is only beyond a particular point that the stress balance becomes negative and Eu-stress turns into distress. The threshold depends on several factors but research has shown the main determinant to be personality type. Responses to stress will depend on:

- expectations;
- past experience;
- personality;
- beliefs;
- vulnerabilities;
- resources;
- knowledge;
- values; and
- drives.

'Persona' was a term used by the ancient Greeks to mean a mask. It later referred to the different roles played by an individual in different situations. The term now denotes the set of characteristics that make a person unique. Each individual has thoughts, feelings, perceptions and so on that together determine the way in which the person responds to external events. Over the centuries attempts have been made by many psychologists to categorize people according to their personalities. Hypocrites grouped people according to their physical shapes, whereas Jung suggested that personalities could be assessed on an introvert–extrovert scale and maintained that those who tended towards introversion were more prone to stress. A more recent theory proposes that individuals can be classified as having more Type A or Type B tendencies.

Do you tear your hair out in traffic jams? Are you constantly analysing queues to decide which is the shortest or which is being served by the most efficient cashier, and still feel annoyed that you joined the 'slow' queue? When you visit a supermarket to purchase three items, and on joining the queue for the express '8 items or fewer' checkout, find that the customer in front of you has nine items, do you become more and more anxious and even contemplate complaining to the cashier, supervisor or manager? If you answered 'yes' to any of these questions, you may tend towards a Type A personality, and will need to look at ways of modifying your hurried and competitive lifestyle. If you answered 'no' you are probably the person with the extra item in the supermarket queue. You are a mostly Type B personality, and are enjoying a fairly relaxed life.

Extreme Type A and Type B personalities find it almost impossible to work together and must realize that none of us has the right to try and 'change' someone else. Questionnaire 2 is designed to find out which personality type the person who completes it exhibits at work.

People with Type A behaviour are continually striving to take and maintain control. This permanent 'strain' correlates with the higher probability of Type A behaviour resulting in cardiovascular disease. (We will look at this in more detail in Chapter 5.)

Studies in the UK show that Type A people have three distinct features:

- they have a strong sense of competition, and are always striving to be in control – this tends to cause some aggression;
- they are strongly committed to their work and immerse themselves fully in their job; and
- they are always working against deadlines and have a sense of time urgency.

Questionnaire 2: Determining personality type

	Yes	No
1 Do you find it difficult to stop work for a tea or coffee break?	☐	☐
2 Do you find it difficult to let your voice-mail or answerphone take your calls even if you are busy doing other work?	☐	☐
3 Do you try to perform several tasks at once (talking to a student, making notes and so on)?	☐	☐
4 Are you constantly wishing that people would hurry up and finish what they are telling you and maybe even finishing their sentences for them?	☐	☐
5 Do you always want to 'get things finished'?	☐	☐
6 Do you perform most tasks at top speed?	☐	☐
7 Do you feel a need to speak at all meetings you attend?	☐	☐
8 Do you have difficulty relaxing?	☐	☐
9 Do you get annoyed with colleagues who have a more relaxed approach to work?	☐	☐
10 Do you find it difficult to laugh at your mistakes?	☐	☐
11 Do you find it difficult to delegate and not interfere?	☐	☐
12 Is it difficult to accept that you will not always be able to do things your way?	☐	☐

Add up the numbers of 'Yes' and 'No' answers. A total of six or more 'Yes' answers indicates that you tend towards Type A behaviour; the more 'Yes' answers you have given, the more Type A personality traits you exhibit.

People demonstrating typical Type A personality traits:

- are very competitive;
- have aggressive speech;
- have a strong personality;
- are easily bored;
- talk, walk and eat quickly;
- finish sentences for others and demonstrate impatience;
- are polyphasic;
- are easily angered;
- cannot relax;
- are forgetful;
- are materialistic;
- find it difficult to work with other Type A personalities;
- are aggressive;
- are tense;
- rush; and
- measure success by gain.

Most organizations would value Type A behaviour. The problems arise, however, when more and more work and responsibility are the reward for the person's dedication, because the senior staff realize that this person will ensure the work is completed to a high standard.

Individuals with Type A personalities should realize that their behaviour is counter-productive. As well as being inefficient when their stress levels are high, they invariably suffer marital and social relationship problems. This is inevitable, as they work longer and longer hours striving to attain their goals. Unfortunately there are only 24 hours in the day, so as more hours are devoted to work, fewer are available for social activities.

If you are Type A at work and getting stressed, chill out.

- Ask your colleagues for their views and be willing to try out their ideas. Be flexible.
- Keep your work separate from other sections of your life.
- Delegate – people like being asked to help. How can they get experience if you won't let them try?
- Stop trying to control everything. Relax.
- Make sure each working day has 'free' time scheduled. Go for a walk at lunch time or go for a meal with colleagues but *do not talk shop*. Take breaks.
- Tell others how you are feeling. They cannot help if they are not aware!

Individuals with Type B personalities display very different traits and have a much more relaxed attitude towards life. They:

- are ambitious but relaxed about it
- are easy going
- go about things slowly and methodically
- play for fun
- are content
- relax
- are slow to anger
- are efficient
- enjoy periods of relaxation; and
- display none of the characteristics of Type A.

Clearly Type B individuals are not preoccupied with their achievements and seldom lose their temper and become angry. They can enjoy their free time and work calmly and smoothly.

We all find ourselves somewhere between the two extremes and our 'type' will change depending on the circumstances. We may be Type A in work but Type B at home or when playing sport, for example.

As well as our personality types, cultural differences also affect our ability to cope with stress. In Japanese society, people are encouraged to accept problems and not fight against them. Problems are perceived as motivators and induce stress as opposed to distress. In the Western world, workers are expected to take control of a problem and solve it rapidly. This immediately places the individual under immense pressure and often results in high stress levels.

Kobasa (1979) suggests that it is the presence of a 'hardiness' factor that prevents individuals from developing both mental and physical illnesses as a result of experiencing stress. She suggested that the 'hardiness' factor be made up of three components: challenge, commitment and control. Challenge refers to the ability to face up to threatening situations in a positive way, commitment refers to the degree of involvement an individual displays in different situations and control means the self-discipline a person has in any situation. The higher the individual scores on these variables, the higher the probability that they will not develop stress-related illnesses.

Many psychologists (Dobson 1982) express the view that the individual's attitude towards stress is important. It is suggested that those who believe they have stressful jobs will experience more stress than others with more positive attitudes. The social class of the individual has also been found to have an effect on the stress level. Gove (1972) found that symptoms associated with clinical depression were more pronounced in working-class women than in women from a middle-class background. This fact was generally attributed to the different sources of stress for people from different backgrounds. For example, it was found that the threat of redundancy caused a high level of stress to those from working-class backgrounds, whereas a high noise level and poor working conditions had a high level of stress for middle-class employees.

Cooper and Payne (1994) suggest that some individuals produce stress for themselves. Some people, they say, will worry about situations that may never happen, whereas others have imagined sources of stress, such as suspicions concerning their partner's fidelity.

It is evident, therefore, that we all have different stress levels and that no two people will react to a situation in exactly the same way. This makes it impossible to determine an appropriate level of stress to optimize performance for any group of workers and understanding needs to be given to those having difficulty coping.

3

GENERAL SOURCES OF STRESS

Most workers are rational and realistic, and accept that their working environments will never be perfect. There are responsibilities and demands associated with all types of work and it is inevitable that these will cause some stress for employees. The challenging, difficult and demanding aspects of work elicit better performance while enhancing self-esteem and enriching the individual's self-identity. However, evidence suggests that many in the UK workforce are suffering very high and, therefore, unacceptable stress levels. Distress is neither a natural nor inevitable consequence of life or work. In this chapter I will discuss the factors that appear to be the cause of that distress.

The levels of stress that become harmful are, according to Worksafe, Western Australia (WWA) (1999), likely to occur when there is:

- prolonged or increasing pressures occurring without relief;
- a sense of powerlessness over the demands being made;
- a series of conflicting demands without easy resolution;
- a continuous threat of violent or aggressive behaviour with little or no defence; and
- organizational change that impacts on individuals.

It can be started, or made worse, they suggest by:

- the presence of bullying, conflict, harassment or indifference and contempt to staff needs;
- the organization lacking leadership and a clear direction;
- work arrangements, deadlines and demands set without consultation and seen to be inflexible; and
- staff experiencing a high degree of uncertainty about their direction, purpose, objectives and job.

Figure 3.1 Organizational sources of stress

More specifically, research has shown that occupational stress results from:

- change;
- work conditions;
- workload;
- role issues;
- relationships at work;
- career development;
- home–work interface;
- job insecurity; and
- management issues.

Sources of stress

Change

Following their research into stress and illness, Holmes and Rahe (1967) produced a list of the 43 events in life that require the individual to readjust. The events are presented in rank order with the 'death of a spouse' being the factor requiring most readjustment by the widow(er) and being credited with 100 Life Change Units (LCU). By looking at Table 3.1 you can quickly calculate how many of these events have happened to you in the past year. The higher their combined rating, the more likely it is that you will experience the manifestations of stress. It is interesting to note that many of the life events listed are pleasant occasions but because they require you to adjust, they can still cause stress. This helps to explain why 'change' has been shown to be the main cause of stress.

It is of paramount importance that everyone learns to cope with change, because it has become a way of life and it cannot be eliminated.

Table 3.1 The social readjustment rating scale (adapted from Holmes and Rahe 1967)

Rank	Life event	Mean value
1	Death of spouse	100
2	Divorce	73
3	Marital separation	65
4	Jail term	63
5	Death of a close family member	63
6	Personal injury or illness	53
7	Marriage	50
8	Fired at work	47
9	Marital reconciliation	45
10	Retirement	45
11	Change in health of family member	44
12	Pregnancy	40
13	Sex difficulties	39
14	Gain of new family member	39
15	Business readjustment	39
16	Change in financial state	38
17	Death of close friend	37
18	Change to different line of work	36
19	Change in number of arguments with spouse	35
20	Large mortgage or loan	31
21	Foreclosure of mortgage or loan	30
22	Change in responsibilities at work	29
23	Son or daughter leaving home	29
24	Trouble with in-laws	29
25	Outstanding personal achievement	28
26	Wife begins or stops work	26
27	Begin or end school	26
28	Change in living conditions	25
29	Revision of personal habits	24
30	Trouble with boss	23
31	Change in work hours or conditions	20
32	Change in residence	20
33	Change in schools	20
34	Change in recreation	19
35	Change in church activities	19
36	Change in social activities	18
37	Small mortgage or loan	17
38	Change in sleeping habits	16
39	Change in number of family get-togethers	15
40	Change in eating habits	15
41	Vacation	13
42	Christmas	12
43	Minor violations of the law	11

The impact of life events and changes on our stress levels will depend to some extent on:

- whether we have previous experience of the event or change;
- if the event or change was predicted; and
- the importance we place on the life event and change.

When growing up, we are all faced with important decisions for the first time: such as whether to study GCSEs in languages or sciences; which university or college to apply to; which career path to follow; whether to leave home, and so on. Later in life, faced with the same choices, we could call upon our experiences to help make our decisions. At some point in our life cycle we have to face the death of a loved one. This is traumatic but normally, somehow or another, we manage to cope and the next time we have to deal with death, although it will still be extremely stressful, we will have developed some coping skills.

The message here is clear: we have to become change-skilled. This, however, is no easy task for most of us. For example, I frequently meet people who tell me that they want to change their lives. Often they inform me that if only they could 'earn a promotion', or 'lose weight', or 'give up smoking' and so on, they would be happy and not stressed. It is then my normal practice to ask them to make one very small change in their lives until they are due to see me again. This minor alteration to their lifestyle could be anything from sitting in a different chair to watch television, to sleeping on the other side of the bed. Usually, at our next meeting, they tell me that they could only keep to the new regime for a few days and had to revert. Until we become flexible and skilled at coping with such minor changes, how can we hope or expect to change our lives?

Working conditions

High levels of background noise at work can not only impair your concentration but can be responsible for irritability, tension and headaches. Workers exposed to high noise levels have been found to be more susceptible to allergies, and respiratory and cardiovascular disorders (Jones 1983). Most blue and white collar workers are not exposed to permanently high levels of noise but if they work in shared offices the sound of a colleague talking on the telephone could be sufficient to cause stress in situations that require total concentration.

Fluorescent lighting can be tiring, and any illumination that is too dim or too bright may cause eye strain and increase fatigue. Artificial light is made up of fewer wavelengths of light than sunlight, and does not cause the same release of chemicals in the body that brings a feeling of emotional well being as sunlight.

Similarly, poor air quality can cause discomfort, which leads to stress. Smoking, overcrowding, pollution and excessive humidity or dryness can contribute to the problem and efforts should be made to ensure that the air is not polluted. This can be a real problem where a room is in constant use by large numbers of people. A lecture theatre, for example, is likely to accommodate over 100 people for each hour of the day. Clearly, if there is no air-conditioning and/or humidifiers and no access to fresh air, those groups that have classes later in the day will be expected to function in a 'stuffy' atmosphere.

Workload

High levels of occupational stress may result when an employee is asked to perform tasks for which they believe they do not have the necessary skills and/or knowledge. It can be equally frustrating if they are not asked to practise the skills they do have. This will lead to boredom and dissatisfaction.

Work overload occurs when the quantity of work expected (output) is at variance with that person's perception of how much they can handle efficiently. Such overload has the potential of lowering the worker's self-esteem because of their own perceived inefficiency. It is perhaps highly significant that the Japanese have a word devoted to the issue, *Karoshi*, which means death from overwork. It was officially recognized as a fatal disease in Japan in 1987.

In 1996 the UK Trades Union Congress (TUC) surveyed safety representatives through their unions to determine the factors that caused most concern. They found that the most commonly reported problems were 'occupational stress' and 'work overload' and suggested that this confirms that the health of British workers is at risk because of the current 'hire and fire' culture. The results of the survey (TUC 1996) showed that stress and overwork affect workers in all sizes of organization and in both the public and private sectors. Education was ranked second in the stress ratings, with 80 per cent of representatives from this sector identifying it as a major problem.

As Table 3.2 shows, the quality of the work is as instrumental as the workload in causing high stress.

Some theorists propose that increasing the employee's locus of control will significantly reduce the level of stress they experience because of their work. The concept refers to the extent to which the individual perceives they have control over a given situation. Someone with an

Table 3.2 Types of workload stress

Quality overload	The employee does not feel capable of undertaking a given task
Quality underload	The task allocated does not make use of the skills and knowledge of the employee
Quantity overload	The employee has too much to do in too little time
Quantity underload	The employee has too little to do (unlikely, but it does occur)

inner locus of control believes they have control over what happens. The individual with an external locus of control, however, appears to be unable to deal with frustration, is more anxious and less concerned with achievement. Compliant and conforming internals like to be in control and resist efforts to be manipulated (McKenna 1987).

When we feel in control, stress becomes a challenge and is no longer a threat. When we lack control, stress can become illness. Marmot *et al.* (1978) conducted research into stress in civil servants. Their study showed that those in the highest grades had the lowest incidence of coronary heart disease; the incidence for those in the lowest grades was four times higher. Employees on the middle scales had 2–3.2 times the incidence of the top grades. One theory that might explain this result is that the more control an individual has over events, the less stress they will experience.

Theorell (1989) states that there are two main areas of work that are relevant to control:

- the degree of authority a worker has over decisions; and
- skill discretion, where the worker has some control over the utilization of their skills and an opportunity to acquire more.

He concludes that a combination of these two factors is directly correlated with health.

Role issues

Role conflict arises when an employee has to play roles that, by their very nature, are not compatible (see Fig. 3.2). An individual who is ambitious and wishes to comply with a request to attend a two-day residential training programme may face a dilemma if they have domestic commitments that they cannot ignore, such as looking after

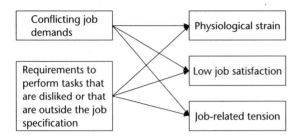

Figure 3.2   Role conflict

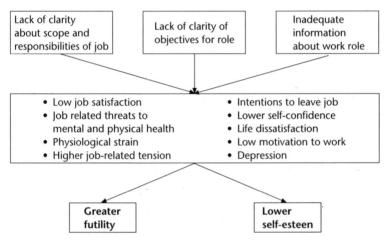

Figure 3.3   Role ambiguity

children. Such conflict may also occur when a person has to 'wear two hats'. A line manager with responsibility for ensuring targets are met will often have to reprimand staff for inefficiency or poor time keeping. This manager may also be accountable for the general welfare of the staff and have empathy for the member of staff being reprimanded through awareness of their domestic problems.

The other major cause of role stress is role ambiguity, which is often the result of an inadequate job description. The worker needs to receive clarification concerning their job and the incumbent responsibilities. As Figure 3.3 shows, role ambiguity occurs when a worker is expected to perform their duties without receiving adequate details about the scope and responsibilities of the job.

Relationships at work

The people we work with can be an important source of both stress and support. Stress among co-workers can arise from competition, personality conflicts and 'office politics'. Ferris *et al.* define office politics as behaviour that produced conflict and ill feeling in the work place by 'putting individuals and/or groups against one another or against the organization' (1996: 234). Office politics are more likely to be found in organizations where resources are scarce. In colleges, for example, where opportunities for promotion are considered a valued organizational resource, there is often a high degree of competitiveness, which can lead to hostility and a very poor working atmosphere.

It has been shown that stress among managers and subordinates usually arises from the inability to delegate, unfair criticism, 'favouritism' and pulling rank unnecessarily.

The Ministry of Labour in Japan conducted a survey that revealed that 52 per cent of women workers had experienced anxiety and stress and the main cause given was unsatisfactory working relationships. One reason for poor working relationships is social or physical isolation, where the individual feels that they lack social support. Another reason could be a poor working relationship with senior staff or peer groups.

In some cases, an employee can be suffering because of the vindictive behaviour of a colleague; sometimes to the extent of harassment and bullying. Work place bullying is defined by the Manufacturing, Science and Finance Union (cited in Ellis 1997) as 'Persistent, offensive, abusive, intimidating, malicious or insulting behaviour, abuse of power or unfair penal sanctions which make the recipient feel upset, threatened, humiliated or vulnerable, which undermines their self-confidence and which may cause them to suffer stress'. Until recently, bullying in the work place has been largely unrecognized by the UK government, employers and, indeed, trade unions, although research conducted by the University of Manchester Institute of Science and Technology (UMIST) found that between a third and half of all stress related illness is directly attributable to work place bullying. The Institute of Personnel Development reported that one in eight employees in the UK have been bullied at work during 1989–94.

Work place bullying can take many forms, such as sexual or racial harassment, but it is generally the result of the abuse of power. If the bully is in a senior position within the organization, the person suffering has the additional problem of ensuring that their complaint is not suppressed; they may have to report to the senior member of staff as part of the grievance procedure. Peer groups may find it difficult to believe that Mr or Ms X is harassing a colleague if they always find the person kind and considerate. This can cause a further lowering of the harassed person's self-esteem.

Idealistically, those in education should be some of the least likely to abuse their power over their subordinates, as this would be the antithesis of the motivations that made them join the profession. Sadly, this is not the case. In the UK the National Association of Schoolmasters/Union of Women Teachers (NAS/UWT) and National Association of Teachers in Further and Higher Education (NATFHE) have published cases where their members were bullied at work.

It is absolutely critical that any employee who is being bullied should feel self-confident about reporting the situation. Too often the victim is afraid to make an official complaint because of the possible repercussions. The organization should ensure that the victim receives adequate counselling. Not only will this reinforce the fact that management is interested in their welfare and thus prevent a further decline in morale and motivation, but it may be extremely cost effective if the victim pursues a personal injury claim.

Good working relationships with peers, subordinates and management are essential to the smooth functioning of any organization. Once established, they act as a support and serve as a buffer against stress.

Career development

Several career issues can act as a source of stress. These may include:

- job insecurity;
- over promotion;
- under promotion; and
- thwarted ambition.

Research shows that individuals suffering from career stress often show poor work performance, job dissatisfaction, burnout and unsatisfactory interpersonal relationships at work.

Today's society places a great deal of emphasis on achievement and the ability to succeed in all aspects of life. Some people might regard themselves as failures if they are unable to live up to one of their particular expectations, whereas others would view failure in only one area as a great success. Self-esteem is the value that individuals place on themselves in terms of previous behaviour (Gelfand 1962) and someone with low self-esteem may despair. It is therefore vital that employees are helped to set realistic goals for themselves.

Reasonable ambition is laudable but if it becomes unrealistic it is likely to result in much stress and anxiety. Researchers claim that over-competitiveness is often the source of mental breakdown and depression. Workers who, at the start of their careers, thought they would become line managers or company directors may have to accept that they are not going to achieve this goal.

Society also finds conscientiousness and hard work commendable. Those who are afraid that they may appear to be anything less than industrious run the risk of becoming obsessive about work. Workaholics can expect to see deterioration in their mental and physical health, as stress and strain will manifest once they realize they can no longer cope effectively at that pace. To seek excellence is an admirable aim in life but to constantly strive after standards that are beyond one's capabilities will lead to personal defeat and a lowering of self-esteem (Dobson 1982).

Anxiety, according to Ellis (1962), is caused by having unrealistic desires or beliefs. He identified five of these as:

- the desire to perform at one's optimum level at all times – clearly this is not an achievable aim as everyone has good and bad days;
- the belief that it is always external factors that cause misfortune;
- the desire to control people and situations so that everything is run in the manner you want;
- the belief that previous bad experiences will 'shape' future events; and
- the desire to be liked, loved or admired by others.

When people accept jobs, they usually do so in the hope and belief that some of their career aspirations will be met. For many workers these aspirations include a desire to learn new skills and acquire new knowledge, and thus advance their careers at the same time as gaining more autonomy.

Much research has been conducted into the effects of career development on the worker. If an individual cannot make use of and develop their skills, their career can stagnate, which can cause high stress (Margolis *et al.* 1974). Similarly, limited career opportunity causes frustration and a lowering of motivation. In today's economic climate there are fewer opportunities to move to other organizations to gain career advancement. This affects the more junior employees, as there are often no internal promotion opportunities until senior staff leave.

Certain groups will suffer stress due to under-promotion. Women are more likely than men to be at lower levels in most organizations, even though they are often more qualified.

Home–work interface

Leading researchers hold different views on the home–work connection. One school of thought suggests that a person with a low self-esteem and low level of satisfaction in work will have similar experiences in their social life. Conversely, compensation theorists believe that positive events in one field compensate for negative or distressing experiences in the other. Perhaps, however, the most applicable view when assessing the impact of the home–work connection on levels of stress is conflict theory. Supporters of this theory believe that work and home are totally incompatible and that one of the variables will always have to suffer if the other is to gain benefit. This can be exemplified in dual-career stress where both partners have careers outside the home limiting the amount of time they can spend on domestic matters. A balance is needed and each individual needs to ensure that an appropriate amount of time is afforded to home life and work life.

Job insecurity

Professor Cary Cooper has been quoted (Hope 1999) as saying that 'Stress caused by work is the new Millennium illness'. This, he states, is a result of the Americanization of the British economy, which has led to short-term contracts, which, in turn lead to job insecurity and long hours of work. Everyone is finding it difficult to secure appropriate employment and many feel that they cannot afford to risk moving to a new location unless more job security is on offer. This in turn causes people to remain in positions they have out-grown; the consequences are frustration and stress.

Management issues

A person's work and occupational stature may play an important role in their sense of identify, self-esteem and psychological well-being.

Locke (1976) outlined six conditions that lead to job satisfaction for a worker. They are:

- work must be mentally stimulating and provide challenges that can be met;
- it should include physical exertion and activity but should not be over tiring;
- the rewards must be just, fair and indicative of performance;

- the work environment should facilitate work goals and should be physically compatible with worker needs;
- work should enhance self-esteem and enrich self-identity in the work force; and
- work leaders and supervisors should facilitate the work process and work goal attainment.

If some or all of these criteria are not met, dissatisfaction with the job may result, the consequences of which are: ill-effects of physical and psychological health; poor labour relations and productivity; high labour turnover and absenteeism; and perhaps a high accident rate. Those occupying managerial positions shoulder the responsibility for ensuring that the six conditions are met. Additionally, they must appreciate that they are managing not a group of workers, but a number of individuals. In particular, they must recognize that their various backgrounds, experience, personalities, and so on, will influence their subordinates to view situations differently.

The UK Health and Safety Executive (HSE) commissioned the University of Bristol to conduct a survey into the causes and levels of stress in different occupational groups. The interim findings, released on 20 May 1999, showed that at least one in five workers are suffering extreme stress because of poor working conditions, long working hours and lack of support (Health and Safety Executive 1999). Of the 4000 volunteers taking part in the study, 25 per cent report that they have experienced physical and/or mental health problems that they attributed to work place pressure.

Management should ensure that workers feel a sense of belonging and that they are encouraged to participate in decision making. An efficient communication system is paramount to the smooth running of the organization and for keeping staff morale at its optimum level.

In summary, it can be seen that the factors that cause high levels of occupational stress can usually be attributed to a lack of control in association with unsatisfied needs, over- or under-stimulation, role conflicts, lack of support, excessive demands and lack of recognition. If we are exposed to them we are likely to experience a dysphoric emotional reaction (anxiety, depression, apathy and so on), which may cause us to behave differently, and possibly, as a consequence, suffer both physical and mental ill health.

4

SOURCES OF STRESS IN FURTHER AND HIGHER EDUCATION

Having looked at stress at a general level, we will now turn to stress in further education (FE) and higher education (HE). Perhaps we can examine some of the theories put forward earlier to test if they apply to lecturers working in these sectors.

Clearly there will be specific constraints, limitations and effects peculiar to this sector but lessons learned from a general study can be applied. Stress in the work place is an all consuming generic term. Stress in FE and HE is a specific phenomenon influenced by specific circumstances in the education sector. Questionnaire 3 is designed for lecturing staff – not for managers at senior levels. Stress at 'top' levels needs a separate study.

One way to start to look at stress in lecturers is to examine the external pressures that are exerted on them in colleges and universities. This is not to say that all these pressures cause stress, but they do affect those who work in FE and HE, although not always, perhaps, at lecturer level. We will also consider stress caused by the modern student and employer. Students are now vociferous, and likely to be aware of 'their rights'. Complaints are easier to make than they once were, and more likely to be given a forum in which they will be heard. Boards of study comprising staff and students meet regularly to discuss the operation of courses and programmes; grievances can be aired and staff are made aware in open forum of students' perceptions and views. To try to encapsulate these pressures, it may help if we view all external forces as being capable of 'pulling strings' on a puppet, the puppet being the lecturer (Fig. 4.1).

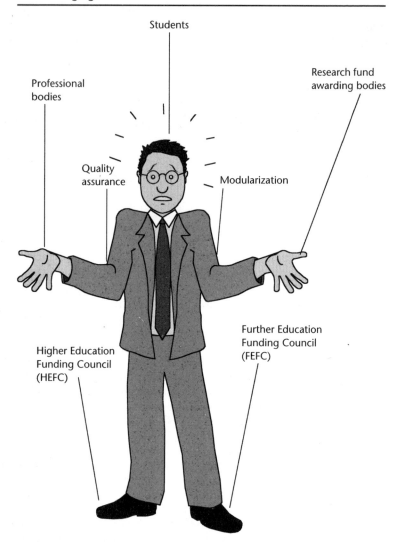

Figure 4.1 Everyday pressures on a lecturer

Given that the FE and HE sector is extremely broad, we must firstly recognize that to some organizations some external bodies are more relevant than others. It is not easy to see an area of common ground between an Oxbridge don and an FE lecturer, and, arguably, there is little common ground between a 'new' university lecturer and a lecturer in a research-led, 'old' university. Factors that cause stress for one do not necessarily cause stress for the other. Top and middle management cannot shield lecturers from pressure, and therefore stress, from external bodies. A quality assurance visit directly involves lecturers, as do the demands made by professional bodies, and students and employers will clearly affect the daily roles of all academic staff.

In the UK in recent years the sector as a whole has seen many changes. Polytechnics and some colleges have become universities. Employment contracts are not with local education authorities, but with the universities and colleges themselves. Holiday arrangements have effectively been reduced. Colleges have merged. Most readers will be able to add to this list. Enterprise is the culture and management structures have been modified significantly in accordance with this. No doubt, each item on our list causes stress and, cynically, we can encapsulate them all by saying 'FE and HE lecturing is not what it was'. No doubt this is true, but it is not entirely useful as an analytical tool.

We are not comparing stress levels today with what they once were. Instead we are looking at stress now to inform ourselves of current causes and symptoms, and means of removing it. Many of the changes mentioned above have a 'life cycle'. Some changes, like corporate status, affected colleges at the same time. Other changes have been more incremental and introduced to suit the institution. Not many colleges now have subject based departments with a single head reporting to the principal. Matrix structures with functional heads are more in vogue, with sometimes less clear lines of authority and responsibility for lecturing staff. How much stress is created will vary between colleges and between staff. Sub-optimal and dysfunctional performance caused by any structure must increase the tendency for stress. Many studies show that the process of change is stressful even if the change, once implemented, does not constantly recreate the stress.

These are then a few, and only a few, comments about the FE and HE sector to give a context to the questionnaire that follows. Let us now try to determine the main factors that cause you most stress as a lecturer.

Questionnaire 3: Sources of work stress for lecturers

Please circle the number that relates to the level of stress you experience due to each factor.

	No stress		Some stress		Extreme stress	
1 Long hours spent preparing and marking work	0	1	2	3	4	5

	No stress		Some stress		Extreme stress	
2 Having too many roles, for example lecturer, counsellor, administrator	0	1	2	3	4	5
3 Being responsible for others	0	1	2	3	4	5
4 Conflicts with colleagues	0	1	2	3	4	5
5 Poor promotion prospects	0	1	2	3	4	5
6 Poor staff development	0	1	2	3	4	5
7 Lack of encouragement outside college	0	1	2	3	4	5
8 Work overload	0	1	2	3	4	5
9 Uncertainty of what is expected of you	0	1	2	3	4	5
10 Too many different demands on your time	0	1	2	3	4	5
11 Relationships with senior colleagues	0	1	2	3	4	5
12 Not having the skills and, therefore, the confidence to do your job	0	1	2	3	4	5
13 Poor communication in the college	0	1	2	3	4	5
14 Having to take work home	0	1	2	3	4	5
15 Having to cope with continuous change at work	0	1	2	3	4	5
16 Poor appraisal system	0	1	2	3	4	5
17 Having to be responsible for making decisions	0	1	2	3	4	5
18 Lack of support from senior management	0	1	2	3	4	5
19 Job insecurity	0	1	2	3	4	5
20 Poor resources	0	1	2	3	4	5
21 Difficulty relaxing outside college	0	1	2	3	4	5
22 Work underload	0	1	2	3	4	5

	No stress		Some stress		Extreme stress	
23 Not having sufficient information made available to do your work properly	0	1	2	3	4	5
24 Dealing with student complaints and appeals	0	1	2	3	4	5
25 Attending social events	0	1	2	3	4	5
26 Salary	0	1	2	3	4	5
27 Low morale in the college	0	1	2	3	4	5
28 The effects of your job on your personal life	0	1	2	3	4	5
29 Coping with student problems such as failure, bereavement	0	1	2	3	4	5
30 Having no clear goal to work towards	0	1	2	3	4	5
31 Administrative work	0	1	2	3	4	5
32 Relationships with colleagues/peers	0	1	2	3	4	5
33 Not being able to use all of your skills and abilities	0	1	2	3	4	5
34 Restrictions on your behaviour, such as dress codes	0	1	2	3	4	5
35 Changes/problems outside work	0	1	2	3	4	5
36 Meeting deadlines	0	1	2	3	4	5
37 Lack of motivation at college	0	1	2	3	4	5
38 Having responsibility for students' futures	0	1	2	3	4	5
39 Lack of social contact to share ideas with	0	1	2	3	4	5
40 Senior staff not appreciating your contribution to the college	0	1	2	3	4	5
41 Responsibility without authority	0	1	2	3	4	5

	No stress		Some stress		Extreme stress	
42 Prioritizing college and home life	0	1	2	3	4	5
43 Fear of making mistakes	0	1	2	3	4	5
44 Working for different course directors – having to work differently for different people	0	1	2	3	4	5
45 College politics	0	1	2	3	4	5
46 'Rivalry' for promotion	0	1	2	3	4	5
47 Poor job satisfaction	0	1	2	3	4	5
48 Poor college environment	0	1	2	3	4	5
49 Personal relationships	0	1	2	3	4	5

Scoring

Enter your score for each question and then add the totals for each column.

Quantity/ quality of college work	Role issues	Level of responsibility/ authority	Social relationships	Job satisfaction	College concerns	Domestic concerns
1 __	2 __	3 __	4 __	5 __	6 __	7 __
8 __	9 __	10 __	11 __	12 __	13 __	14 __
15 __	16 __	17 __	18 __	19 __	20 __	21 __
22 __	23 __	24 __	25 __	26 __	27 __	28 __
29 __	30 __	31 __	32 __	33 __	34 __	35 __
36 __	37 __	38 __	39 __	40 __	41 __	42 __
43 __	44 __	45 __	46 __	47 __	48 __	49 __
Totals:						
__	__ __		__	__	__	__

Once you have entered your scores for each question in the boxes, add up the vertical columns to give you a total score for each section. Note which section is causing you most stress (the higher your score the higher the stress) and start thinking about the action you need to take to help you cope with these concerns.

(Adapted from Powell 1992)

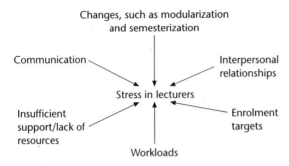

Figure 4.2 Main causes of stress in higher education lecturers

Stress in higher education ◼

Figure 4.2 shows the main sources of stress in lecturing that have been identified in recent years. Let us now take a brief look at each of these in turn.

Change

Although research (Wardell *et al.* 1964) has shown that those with responsibility for people are far more likely to experience stress resulting in heart disease than those with responsibility for property; the role of the lecturer has never been considered by society as one that elicits high levels of occupational stress. However, during the past 20 years or so, academics have witnessed some real changes in their work environment and these changes have resulted in increased workloads, and a decrease in the level of control that lecturers have over their work (Melandez and Guzman 1983). Loss of autonomy has provided the potential for the manifestation of high levels of work stress (Hickcox 1983).

The UK Audit Commission's three Es – economy, effectiveness and efficiency – have placed further pressures on academics. Lecturers are continually reminded to pay attention to quality control and the accompanying administrative work while being asked to undertake more work and more responsibility.

FE and HE establishments work in an increasingly competitive environment, which necessitates them responding to external challenges and pressures at a time when there may be fewer resources available and yet greater expectations of them. The FE and HE sectors have recently undergone numerous changes, such as:

- the modularization of courses and associated assessment requirements;
- changes in the length and organization of the college year; and
- increasing student numbers and the changing profile of the student population, as already discussed.

Insufficient support/lack of resources

Lecturers continually report that they are put under increasing pressure by management without being afforded additional resources to help with their additional tasks. This has been cited by many academics, who found that a management decision to change the traditional college year to a semesterized plan caused a major increase in their workload. Examinations had to be set and marked twice each year instead of once, and assessing and arranging examination boards took up more time. In addition, modularization has meant that it has been more time consuming to track students' progress. Students are at liberty to study a diverse range of subjects (possibly from a variety of faculties), which is clearly more difficult to coordinate for the programme directors or year tutors. These problems are less noticeable in colleges with an efficient computer support unit, where student records can be held on a college database. A recent survey of lecturers in HE employed in Wales, conducted by the author, showed that many academics are generally dissatisfied with the support units present in their organization. Over 50 staff gave actual examples of their discontent, with comments such as: 'The person in charge of our Quality Support Unit criticises all documents that the academic staff write. He offers no help and probably couldn't do any better himself'.

And, of a computer support unit:

> We are asked to fill in forms to enrol students and then to check computer print-outs many times throughout the year, often repeatedly correcting the same errors . . . but when we ask for annual statistics from the unit you can guarantee they will be wrong. Is it any wonder academics are reluctant to give up more of their time on fruitless tasks?

Enrolment targets

Increased competition between educational organizations has placed lecturers under pressure to enrol the target number of students. Failure to achieve this goal could, they are told, result in redundancies. The level of qualifications for acceptance on courses may be lowered in order to meet the target number of students but this often results in a higher student failure rate at the end of the academic year. Lecturers then have to account for this and are held responsible for high wastage levels. According to a survey conducted for Labour Research, over 100 of 275 English colleges which took part in the study made a financial loss last year. This occurred despite the fact that 275 full time lecturing posts had been cut in an attempt to prevent such a loss. In Kingsway College, North London and North Oxfordshire College & School of Art in Banbury, 38 per cent and 37 per cent of staff, respectively, were shed. Student numbers, however, had risen by 13 per cent in the previous four years (*Daily Mail*, 4 August, 1999).

Workload

Lecturers, like other white-collar workers, expect to be given sufficient time to complete tasks to the best of their ability and to be given the opportunity to use their knowledge and skills. Research suggests that these expectations are becoming more and more unlikely to be realized. With fewer staff available and staff recruitment 'frozen' in most colleges, lecturers are not able to work at their best ability and, furthermore, are being required to undertake roles for which they do not consider themselves best qualified.

A survey conducted by the UK Association of University Teachers in 1994 showed that the average academic worked over 53 hours a week and that they spent an average of 17.5 hours a week of their own time on administration. It will come as no surprise to these lecturers in FE and HE that recent surveys have shown that the changes in the profession have resulted in high levels of occupational stress in lecturers. Without some reduction in the stress level, the degenerative process of this stress will seriously affect their coping resources. Additionally, their efficiency and effectiveness in the classroom will be impaired. Another source of stress identified in lecturers employed in HE was having insufficient time to keep abreast of current developments in their field.

Lecturers are now finding research work to be a source of anxiety and distress (Fisher 1994), whereas in the past this was an enjoyable task. Academics are under growing pressure to increase their researching and publishing of refereed articles, conference papers or edited books, which will contribute to the next Research Assessment Exercise, which ultimately decides the amount of funding their institution will receive. This onerous task is creating extreme stress in individuals, who fear job loss if they do not publish sufficient articles (Abouserie 1996). It is also resulting in many instances of interdepartment conflict as well as rivalry between colleagues in the same department. The pressure does not stop here. There are dual and conflicting role demands on the lecturer, which further add to the ever-increasing workload. Many staff will be required to produce quality assessment reports and associated documentation required by the HEFC or FEFC, which assess the quality of the teaching provision. The same staff may also be required to produce annual reports, update existing programmes and write the necessary documents for the validation of proposed new courses. At the same time as these activities are taking place, students will expect (quite rightly) good quality teaching and learning experiences. They may also turn to lecturers for advice regarding any financial or domestic problems they may have. On top of these duties, assignments have to be marked, students selected, research students supervised, work placements found and a multitude of meetings and conferences attended.

Interpersonal relationships

Interpersonal relationships with colleagues (at all levels) and students are often causes of high stress levels, but it is the perceived lack of equity that is reported as being the prime cause of conflict between staff. The reward for conducting your job efficiently is more work. It seems that it is rare for a lecturer to receive a word of praise for good performance but very likely that they will be given more responsibility – usually without an increase in status or financial gain. Staff who are unreliable and do not produce work of such a high standard will be given less work. Inevitably this leads to animosity, particularly where two lecturers are paid the same salary but have very different workloads.

Staff–student relationships are not without their problems. Since the introduction of the Students' Charter there has been an increase in the number of student complaints and appeals. Many lecturers share the view of a Principal Lecturer (PL) in a college of HE who said: 'students now think that they can argue and complain if they do not get the mark they think they deserve'. Each letter of complaint, however unfounded, has to be dealt with, and this entails copious amounts of paperwork that again adds to stress levels.

Communication

In organizations where communication systems are no longer effective, and staff feel that they have little say in how things are run, the staff morale and motivation will decline. In extreme cases, lecturers are given timetables that cannot be negotiated and are required to be present on site for the requisite number of hours. If the lecturer shares an office, the environment is often not conducive for such tasks as marking, and the member of staff would be more efficient if allowed to mark at home. When rules are applied so rigidly, good-will soon disappears. As one female lecturer said: 'They apply factory conditions to professionals . . . If you treat us like shop-floor workers you get shop-floor mentality'.

Stress in further education

The picture does not appear to be any brighter in FE, as the results of a survey show (Snape 1988).

The main areas of concern identified were:

- *Resources* The majority (67 per cent) agreed that the financial cutbacks in the FE sector had impacted on the resources available. In some cases this meant that lecturers were using dated equip-ment that had no relevance to industrial requirements. Staff also felt that it was an impossible task for them to update courses and, indeed, their teaching, unless more money was made available.
- *Student contact* Some lecturers felt threatened when asked to teach new subject areas in order to 'fill' their timetables. The academics also perceived that some stress was due to the low ability level of some students, who disrupted the rest of the class. Lecturers were of the opinion that high unemployment levels had led these students to return to education.
- *Interpersonal relationships with colleagues* The staff perceived a break-down in communications between lecturers and management and each party felt the other had no conception of the other's role. Lecturers felt that they could not air their grievances for fear of discrimination. Poor communications might also contribute to the distinct feeling of inequity where some staff members felt that they were being paid less for doing more.
- *Everyday problems* Poor car-parking facilities, which sometimes resulted in lecturers arriving late for classes, were seen as a serious stressor. Having to share workrooms was problematical for many and 95 per cent of the sample stated they were highly stressed when having to attend meetings that they considered a waste of time. Lunchtime meetings are becoming more common in an effort to overcome the lack of time available during the day for

such events. This dilemma has arisen because of the increased workloads, which diminishes the flexibility of those concerned.

Increased group sizes for such things as tutorials prevent the lecturer from having the opportunity for reinforcing the subject matter, ironing out problems with individuals or having an academic debate with students that both parties find beneficial. Tutorials can eliminate many problems that otherwise would increase the lecturers' stress. For example, one lecturer said she was angry because: 'The personnel manager . . . did not consider dissertation/project supervision as part of the contracted class time. As well as the potential for work overload, the lack of recognition of the value and work of this type of exercise was extremely stressful to the lecturers who increasingly felt that the non-academic administrative staff were determined to squeeze out every last drop of their academic life-blood'.

Over half of the sample admitted that they were taking increasing amounts of work home. This was partly due to time pressures at work but also due to the unsatisfactory work environment.

Research shows that both male and female academics perceive the structure and content of their professions in a similar way (Doyle and Hind 1998), but whereas women reported a higher general stress level, the results indicate that they actually cope better than their male colleagues with the demands placed upon them. It has been suggested that female lecturers face additional pressures because the vast majority of them work in a context of male dominated management. Women in the profession, they felt, have limited access to promotion and resources (Doyle and Hind 1998). They also suggest that there remains a 'glass ceiling', with women holding more junior positions than men and remaining in them for longer than men do. Their results also indicated that female lecturers who had succeeded in gaining higher posts experienced more stress than men in equivalent positions. Cary Cooper shares these views (Day 1994: 23):

I'm not surprised that women professors work the longest hours. There are so few of them. It's the glass-ceiling effect. Many professional women can see positions at the top but they can't get them . . . so to get to the top and stay there, they have to publish more, work harder and be more active.

Abouserie (1996) showed that 14.7 per cent of the academics were experiencing severe stress, and reported that they may need professional help and support to alleviate their anxiety.

When all of the facts are considered it is little wonder that the main lecturers' professional bodies are so concerned about the welfare of their members: 'Colleges and universities require a highly qualified and flexible workforce, but a high quality service cannot be delivered to students if lecturers are overworked, poorly managed and demonstrate low levels of motivation and morale' (Earley 1994: 20).

5

STRESS AND HEALTH

As seen in Figure 5.1, although stress is common to us all, the ways in which it manifests itself are affected by individual differences such as genetic make-up, experience and developmental and environmental influences. These differences help to explain why a certain situation appears exciting and challenging to one person but extremely daunting and indeed traumatic to another.

Take ten minutes to work through Questionnaire 4, which will help you identify how stress affects you. You can now see how your stress manifests itself. This will help you to become aware of the signs to detect when you are anxious and you will need to refer back to these when we look at the most appropriate methods for dealing with your stress in Chapter 6.

Stress has been estimated to cost the UK over £9 billion each year with over 10 per cent of the workforce suffering high stress levels at any time. It has been suggested that over 18 million working days are lost every year due to mental illness, with stress being the main contributor. When considering these facts some caution does need to be exercised. Views on the social acceptability of absence from work due to mental ill health have changed. More people are willing to admit to a mental illness than ever before but, nevertheless, some

$$\text{Sum effect of your stressor} \div \left(\text{Your coping strategies} + \text{Your personality and background} \right) = \text{Effects of stress}$$

Figure 5.1 Equation showing the determinants of the effects of stress

Questionnaire 4: How stress affects you

Please circle the number that indicates the frequency of the factors.

	Never happens		Sometimes		Always	
1 I get angry very easily with students and colleagues	0	1	2	3	4	5
2 I rarely have any energy or enthusiasm to do my work	0	1	2	3	4	5
3 I drink/smoke/comfort eat more	0	1	2	3	4	5
4 I find it hard to concentrate	0	1	2	3	4	5
5 I cannot relax	0	1	2	3	4	5
6 I never feel very well	0	1	2	3	4	5
7 I cannot get into a regular sleeping pattern	0	1	2	3	4	5
8 I find it difficult to make decisions	0	1	2	3	4	5
9 I tend to be moody	0	1	2	3	4	5
10 I suffer from stomach complaints, such as indigestion, sickness, diarrhoea	0	1	2	3	4	5
11 I try to avoid difficult situations	0	1	2	3	4	5
12 I cannot grasp new ideas	0	1	2	3	4	5
13 I often do not want to enter a classroom and face the students	0	1	2	3	4	5
14 I regularly suffer from migraines/headaches	0	1	2	3	4	5
15 I am not sociable	0	1	2	3	4	5
16 I worry a lot	0	1	2	3	4	5
17 I look on the black side of things	0	1	2	3	4	5

	Never happens		Sometimes		Always	
18 My heart races and my breathing is fast	0	1	2	3	4	5
19 I do not enjoy leisure time	0	1	2	3	4	5
20 I do not have much self-confidence	0	1	2	3	4	5

Scoring

As before (Questionnaire 3), enter your scores for each question in the box and then total each section.

Emotional	Physical	Behavioural	Mental
1———	2———	3———	4———
5———	6———	7———	8———
9———	10———	11———	12———
13———	14———	15———	16———
17———	18———	19———	20———
Totals: ———	———	———	———

(Adapted from Powell 1992)

of the stigma remains. We also need to take into account the associated changes in diagnostic practice and the fact that there may have been changes in the willingness to take time off from work. All of these factors could combine to produce larger reported changes in mental health problems than in those associated with physical health. However, it is unlikely that a contrast of such size could be without some real foundation.

Ill health resulting from stress is now the second most commonly reported work-related illness (Health and Safety Executive 1995) and a survey conducted in 1992 showed that 48 per cent of European workers consider that their health is affected by occupational stress. Just how is our health affected? Let us look at the changes that occur in our bodies when we are stressed. This will help us to understand the reasons we become ill when subjected to extreme pressure.

When we perceive that we cannot cope with a situation, that is, when we are stressed, the master gland in the brain (the hypothalamus) sends hormonal messages to the adrenal glands to produce the stress hormones adrenaline, noradrenalin and cortisol. These hormones help to increase the activity of the sympathetic nervous system, which means that our heart beats faster and our blood pressure, respiration and perspiration rates increase. At the same time, our blood vessels and muscles constrict, which makes us feel tense, our pupils dilate and our hearing becomes more acute.

The release of the stress hormones, in turn, activates the enteric nervous system, which is situated in the stomach and works independently of the brain and central nervous system. This causes us to experience 'butterflies in the stomach' but, in severe cases, irritable bowel syndrome and colitis may result.

Clearly, many physical changes take place when we are stressed and if these cannot be controlled they can cause illnesses that can be classified broadly under two headings: physiological and psychological.

Physiological illnesses

Unfortunately, when stressed, the body uses all of its energy to produce stress hormones and research shows that it will begin to lose the ability to produce the chemicals that protect us from viruses, bacteria etc. The level of impact that stress will have on our immune system will depend upon the nature, duration and frequency of the stressful situations. Some of the illnesses that can be caused or exacerbated by stress are shown in Figure 5.2.

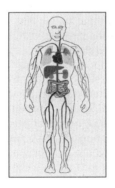

The cardiovascular system
• Hypertension
• Atherosclerosis

The digestive system
• Peptic ulcers
• Gastric ulcers

The immune system
• Allergies: anaphylaxis, urticaria, asthma, hay fever

Figure 5.2 Physiological effects of stress

Psychological stress has also been shown to increase susceptibility to viral infection. Subjects exposed to stress showed increases in infection rates from 74 per cent to 90 per cent, and the incidence of clinical colds rose from 27 per cent to 47 per cent. Earlier studies have shown that medical students have an increased risk of mononucleosis during examination periods. This is not surprising, as stress does suppress the immune system; latent viruses then have an easier time resurging, since the body cannot defend itself as well as usual (Brosschot et al. 1994). This is supported by studies showing that colds and other infections manifest themselves on weekends after busy and stressful work weeks. Additionally, studies on monkeys have shown that ulceration showed up most severely during the rest and recovery periods, rather than during the stress period itself.

When a person is stressed and the immune system is suppressed, latent viruses can become active. However, non-viral diseases such as asthma, diabetes and heart disease have also been shown to be linked to stress. Research suggests that there are emotional factors present in 70 per cent of all asthma cases (see Koenker n.d.). In asthma, a disease that involves both external and internal factors, it is the internal factor that is most affected by acute effects of psychological stressors. Studies have shown that children with chronic asthma improve considerably when away from their parents. The changes may have resulted from removal of an interaction that produced frequent stressful situations as family therapy has been used successfully to treat severe and chronic asthma in children. Additionally, asthmatics exposed to a harmful substance that they thought they were allergic to elicited a severe attack. Even more importantly, interactions between antigens and immunoglobulin E antibodies lead to the release of histamine, which blocks airways, and other mediating agents (Elliot and Eisdorfer 1982). When antigens have an easier time invading the body, as they do under stress, the number of such interactions increases considerably.

Diabetes mellitus, the most common form of diabetes, is significantly affected by stress. Physical or psychological stressors can alter insulin needs; stressors may often be responsible for episodes of loss of control, especially in diabetic children. Type II diabetes is most often affected by stress, as it tends to occur in overweight adults and is a less severe form of diabetes. Additionally, children who had stressful life events stemming from actual or threatened losses within the family and occurring between ages 5 and 9 had a significantly higher risk of Type I diabetes.

Gastrointestinal diseases, such as peptic ulcers and ulcerative colitis, are known to be greatly influenced by stress. Peptic ulcers occur twice as often in air traffic controllers as in civilian co-pilots, and occurred more frequently in the USA among air traffic controllers at high-stress control centres (Chicago O'Hare, La Guardia, JFK and Los Angeles International Airport) than at low-stress control centres (airports in less-populated cities in Virginia, Ohio, Texas and Michigan). Although stress is a major factor in the incidence of peptic ulcers, more than 20 other factors are thought to be associated too: blood type; sex; HLA type; alcoholic cirrhosis; hypertension; chronic obstructive pulmonary disease; cigarette smoking; and even consumption of coffee, carbonated beverages or milk.

Ulcers are caused by excessive stomach acid, and studies of patients with gastric fistulas (openings leading from the stomach to the outside of the body) have shown that anger and hostility increase stomach acidity, while depression and withdrawal decrease it. Stress ulcers frequently occur in patients who experience severe trauma, extensive surgery, major burns or infections, brain injury or surgery, or other catastrophic events. Stress ulcers are quite different from peptic ulcers; they are acute, haemorrhagic (bleeding), and are usually preceded by shock (Stephens 1980). Another effect of stress is the increase in the tendency for blood to coagulate. This leads to a build up of blood platelets causing the blood to have to travel through narrower arteries. This in turn forces the heart to work harder to produce blood flow, and causes a condition known as myocardial ischemia, or hardening of the arteries.

Most people suffer from headaches at one time or another. These may be vascular, such as migraine, which are the most incapacitating, or tension headaches. The latter can be caused by worry, frustration and general lifestyle. The ache occurs when there is insufficient oxygen to feed the contracted muscles in the head and neck, and the blood vessels expand in an attempt to secure a larger oxygen supply.

A detailed explanation of the physiological changes that cause a headache is not required, but it is beneficial to appreciate the association between the pain and the amount of blood flowing in the brain. When an individual is under pressure, the muscles in the neck and head contract. Tense muscles need more oxygen and the blood vessels in the muscles therefore expand to secure a larger supply. Pains can also be felt with the beat of the pulse as the blood flows through the swollen vessels. Most of us will take painkillers to deal with the problem but that really does nothing to develop our coping mechanisms. The analgesic merely acts as a 'mask'. Research has shown that relaxation techniques and biofeedback are the most effective long-term methods for curing tension headaches (this will be discussed later).

In normal situations, the heart beats 72 times every minute and our blood pressure is approximately 100 plus our age (systolic reading) and 80mmHg (diastolic reading). When stressed the heart beats faster and these readings increase. Over a period of time, the probability of a heart attack is considerably increased.

Table 5.1 shows how the different parts of the body are affected by increasing levels of stress experienced by an individual.

In recent years there has been a growing interest in the increase in cardiovascular diseases such as coronary heart disease or stroke. It has been estimated that only approximately 25 per cent of all heart disease could be controlled even if factors such as cholesterol, blood pressure and smoking could be regulated. The development of the remaining 75 per cent of heart disease has been attributed to occupational stress. The British Heart Foundation has estimated that heart disease costs an organization employing 10,000 people approximately £1.6 million for men and £370,000 for women in lost productivity.

The British government stated its intent to reduce coronary heart disease and stroke rates by the year 2000. But according to the Health Education Authority (1988), over 35 million working days are lost each year due to cardiovascular disorders, and about 13 per cent of all male absences are related to coronary heart disease. The UK and Eire have among the worst death rates for coronary heart disease in the world (for males aged 40–69), matched only by Finland and New Zealand. The death rate (for males 40–69) in England and Wales is nine times what it is in Japan. Furthermore, while the rates in certain other countries appear to be decreasing (by 37 per cent for males aged 40–69 in the USA, by 30 per cent in Japan and by 18 per cent in Finland) there is little change in our rates. Fortunately, coronary bypass surgery is now extremely successful and this means that fewer people are dying from cardiovascular disease. Many are, however, forced to retire from work and their quality of life is lessened.

Coronary heart disease is generally associated with factors such as high levels of cholesterol in the blood, a family history of heart problems, high blood pressure, obesity and smoking. It is therefore surprising to learn that none of these factors are found in approximately 50 per cent of all new cases of heart disease. The only acceptable explanation offered to date is that the person's personality type plays a major part in determining the stress levels experienced. Research has shown that individuals with Type A personalities are twice as likely to suffer heart disease than others, and some studies further suggest that Type A individuals will have greater blockage of the arteries. Type A individuals are extremely competitive and try to achieve more than friends and colleagues, and tend to judge themselves by the amount of success – money, assets and friends – that they have rather than the quality of each success.

Table 5.1 Effects of stress on bodily functions (Melhuish 1993)

	Normal (relaxed)	Under pressure	Acute pressure	Chronic pressure (stress)
Brain	Blood supply normal	Blood supply up	Thinks more clearly	Headaches and migraines, tremors and nervous tics
Mood	Happy	Serious	Increased concentration	Anxiety, loss of sense of humour
Saliva	Normal	Reduced	Reduced	Dry mouth, lump in throat
Muscles	Blood supply normal	Blood supply up	Improved performance	Muscular tension and pain
Heart	Normal rate and blood pressure	Increased rate and blood pressure	Improved performance	Hypertension and chest pain
Lungs	Normal respiration	Increased respiration rate	Improved performance	Coughs and asthma
Stomach	Normal blood supply and acid secretion	Reduced blood supply Increased acid secretion	Reduced blood supply reduces digestion	Ulcers due to heartburn and indigestion
Bowels	Normal blood supply and bowel activity	Reduced blood supply Increased bowel activity	Reduced blood supply reduces digestion	Abdominal pain and diarrhoea
Bladder	Normal	Frequent urination	Frequent urination due to increased nervous stimulation	Frequent urination, prostatic symptoms
Sexual organs	(M) Normal (F) Normal periods, etc.	(M) Impotence (decreased blood supply) (F) Irregular periods	Decreased blood supply	(M) Impotence (F) Menstrual disorders
Skin	Healthy	Decreased blood supply, dry skin	Decreased blood supply	Dryness and rashes
Biochemistry	Normal: oxygen consumed, glucose and fats liberated	Oxygen consumption is up. Glucose and fat consumption is up	More energy immediately available	Rapid tiredness

Table 5.2 Type A personality and health

Type A and your health	Physiology of Type A behaviour
You double the risk of heart disease if you score highly as a Type A personality.	
Type A behaviour is associated with:	Type A behaviour leads to:
• stomach ulcers • allergies • exaggerated response of the sympathetic nervous system • poor mental health – anxiety and depression	• excessive discharge of the stress hormones, noradrenaline, adrenaline, cortisol • excess insulin in blood stream • narrowing of blood vessels • increased deposits of clotting material in the blood

Stress Management Research Associates (1998) define Type A individuals as 'hard-driving, competitive, impatient and aggressive. They tend to be achievement striving and hostile'. On the other hand, Type B individuals are more patient and lack the sense of urgency. They tend to be more relaxed and rarely become angry or irritable with themselves or others. More importantly, they know how to relax and enjoy leisure time.

Clearly these are descriptions of two extremes on the continuum, and most of us will be positioned nearer the centre. However, we must not ignore the research conducted by Rosenman and Friedman in the 1950s. They surveyed 3000 healthy adult men and categorized over half as displaying Type A behaviour with the associated high risk of coronary heart disease.

Which group would you consider you fit into? If you exhibit mostly Type A behaviour your health may suffer and there is a real need to find ways of modifying your way of life to reduce the risk of heart failure. (See Table 5.2.)

Psychological illnesses

Three of the more common psychological manifestations of long-term stress are depression, burnout and breakdown, and it has been estimated that in the UK the cost of certified absence from work due to one of these illnesses is £5.3 billion (CBI 1991). It has also been suggested that one in five of the working population will suffer a mental illness each year (O'Leary 1990).

In the UK between 1994 and 1996 there was a 15 per cent increase in women and a 10 per cent increase in men taking anti-depressants (Wilson 1998). It has been estimated that over 75 per cent of patients visiting their GPs have stress-related illnesses. Due to time pressures, the doctors often do not have time to counsel their patients appropriately and many resort to prescribing antidepressants and related medicines. Although these may help to alleviate the symptoms, they do not resolve the underlying problem. In other words, they provide a mask to cover up the effects of the stress but the causes continue to exist and cause more pressure (Looker and Gregson 1997).

Depression

Whereas the cold is the most common physical illness, depression is the mental illness that affects most people (Rosenham and Seligman 1989). Depression is so pervasive that it changes everyday life for the individual concerned. 'Depression is a disturbance in mood, a prolonged emotional state that colours all mental processes' (Rice 1992: 97). A depressed employee has to function feeling hopeless and helpless and the signs and symptoms of Stage 3 stress are evident. It becomes almost impossible to concentrate on work and in many serious cases thought disturbances such as suicidal tendencies and delusions of persecution may result.

The illness tends to trigger increased production of adrenaline and cortisol, which ultimately suppress the immune system. It is not surprising, therefore, that research has shown a direct correlation between the incidence of depression and headaches, asthma, ulcers and coronary heart disease (Friedman and Booth-Kewley 1987).

Depression often manifests as a reaction to personal crises such as bereavement, redundancy, financial loss or divorce. Mitchell, Cronkite and Moos (1983) found that people with severe depression tend to experience high levels of stress in their lives and have fewer personal resources/supports than do their peers who are not depressed.

An important part of the stress management process is recognizing when a problem exists and accepting that there will be occasions when you have to ask for help from others – medics, line managers, family, friends and so on. Most of us suffer from mild depression at some time in our lives. It does help to remember that we all make mistakes and as long as you learn from your mistakes, your failures are no more than a part of your learning process. In other words, positive thinking really can help.

Breakdown

If the individual is under sustained Stage 3 stress for long periods and has become totally exhausted, breakdown point may occur. The onset of this condition may be slow, which is often the case with mental breakdown, but can be fast and severe, as in physical breakdown. The latter may manifest as a stroke or heart attack. Physicians find it difficult to distinguish between unhappiness or depression and breakdown, but it is generally agreed that breakdown occurs when the individual exhibits behaviour that makes it impossible for them to continue functioning normally in society.

Symptoms of a nervous breakdown are often more obvious to others than they are to the sufferer and include:

- obsessive activity such as persistently washing hands or checking that a door is locked;
- manic depression, where there are extreme mood swings;
- behaving irrationally, for example shoplifting, giving up a good job, breaking up good relationships; and
- screaming, shouting and self mutilation.

These are just a few examples. Where breakdown is suspected professional help must be obtained as soon as possible.

Burnout

Burnout is said to occur when individuals who were extremely enthusiastic and conscientious about their jobs appear to lose interest. It is common in hard-working people who become either emotionally, psychologically or physically exhausted. Maslach and Leiter (1997) state that burnout is expressed in three ways:

- an erosion of commitment with the job – the worker loses interest;
- an erosion of emotions where feelings such as happiness, enthusiasm and security are replaced by depression, apathy and anxiety; and
- lack of fit between the person and the job.

Common symptoms of burnout are:

- an increasing tendency to think negatively;
- a feeling of lack of control over events;
- a feeling of being 'useless'; and
- problems with relationships in and out of work.

Frequently, burnout will manifest itself in a lowering of productivity and efficiency and a dissatisfaction with the job. Unfortunately, not all managers view this condition correctly as a psychiatric disorder and interpret the symptoms as laziness and inefficiency. Their handling of the matter, therefore, often exacerbates the situation.

6

STRESS MANAGEMENT

So far we have looked at the signs and symptoms of stress and the factors that are most likely to cause high stress levels in the individual. In this chapter I discuss the ways in which we can learn to control our stress levels and by so doing, develop the skills that will enable us to cope. As Selye (1974: 17) said: 'Contrary to public opinion, we must not, and indeed cannot, avoid stress; we can meet it efficiently and enjoy it by learning about its mechanisms and adjusting our philosophy of life accordingly'.

The information in this section is intended as an introduction to some of the many methods that can be used to reduce stress levels. It aims to provide enough information to enable you to decide which might suit you best. You then need to gather more details and/or enrol at a suitable class for professional instruction.

Stress management shares its main aim with the National Health Service: to prevent physical, mental and emotional illness. Once you have mastered the art of stress management, you will:

- be able to function effectively and efficiently, even when under pressure;
- improve the quality of your life; and
- avoid the ill health associated with high levels of long-term stress.

It is unfortunate that in most instances individuals tend to look for a 'quick fix'. Medications are increasingly the first line of help for those suffering high stress levels, but they do not provide a long-term solution. In addition, they may become habit-forming and/or produce side effects. They can, however, be valuable as short-term solutions to the problem while other curative methods are being introduced.

In the 1990s most newspapers, magazines and counsellors have advised us all to take time out and relax, have a massage, listen to soothing music and to try a variety of other techniques. It is now becoming clear that it is not possible to offer blanket advice as we all differ in the ways we react to short-term and long-term stress and will, therefore, have to develop our own coping mechanisms. If, for example a particular class has been very difficult, some lecturers will feel the need to tell colleagues in the next break, whereas others will remain quiet and internally reflect on the problem. While there is no panacea, there are improvements that can be made in almost all situations. Measures can be adopted to hold stress at acceptable levels and, therefore, minimize its harmful effects. Before looking at these, complete Questionnaire 5 to determine how you currently cope when faced with high stress levels.

Questionnaire 5: How do you cope?

Please circle the number that best describes your way of coping over the past 2 months.

	Never		Sometimes		Frequently	
1 Request help from others	0	1	2	3	4	5
2 Talk about my worries	0	1	2	3	4	5
3 Manage my time so that I am not rushed	0	1	2	3	4	5
4 Remain objective, not taking things personally	0	1	2	3	4	5
5 Enjoy hobbies and leisure activities	0	1	2	3	4	5
6 Stay physically fit with exercises and healthy diet	0	1	2	3	4	5
7 Put things off	0	1	2	3	4	5
8 Delegate wherever possible	0	1	2	3	4	5
9 Look for advice and information from superiors	0	1	2	3	4	5

	Never		Sometimes		Frequently	
10 Work towards set goals and objectives	0	1	2	3	4	5
11 Stand back and think things through	0	1	2	3	4	5
12 Keep home and work separate	0	1	2	3	4	5
13 Treat myself to something pleasurable (gifts, clothes, food)	0	1	2	3	4	5
14 Withdraw from people – bottle things up	0	1	2	3	4	5
15 Say 'No' to extra work – refuse requests	0	1	2	3	4	5
16 Spend time with supportive family and friends	0	1	2	3	4	5
17 Plan ahead (days, weeks, months, years)	0	1	2	3	4	5
18 Have realistic expectations about myself, accepting my limitations	0	1	2	3	4	5
19 Become absorbed in rewarding or creative activity outside work	0	1	2	3	4	5
20 Make time for periods of planned deliberate relaxation (lunchtime, evenings, weekends, holidays)	0	1	2	3	4	5
21 Work longer hours	0	1	2	3	4	5
22 Express emotions openly and directly	0	1	2	3	4	5
23 Confide work problems to partner/close friend	0	1	2	3	4	5
24 Set priorities and make lists of things to do	0	1	2	3	4	5

	Never		Sometimes		Frequently	
25 Accept situations that cannot be altered	0	1	2	3	4	5
26 Relax and 'turn off' at home	0	1	2	3	4	5
27 Find comfort in spiritual activity and contemplation	0	1	2	3	4	5
28 Increase intake of alcohol, cigarettes, drugs or food	0	1	2	3	4	5

Scoring

Assertiveness	Social support	Self-organization	Rationality	Hobbies/leisure	Self-care	Maladaptive
1 __	2 __	3 __	4 __	5 __	6 __	7 __
8 __	9 __	10 __	11 __	12 __	13 __	14 __
15 __	16 __	17 __	18 __	19 __	20 __	21 __
22 __	23 __	24 __	25 __	26 __	27 __	28 __
Totals: __	__	__	__	__	__	__

(Adapted from Powell 1992)

Stress at work is affected by:

- the level of control the employee has over the pressures of work;
- the support they receive from others in meeting the pressures; and
- the strategies they use to respond to the pressures.

Your scores will tell you the current method(s) you use to try and reduce your anxiety. Hopefully you have no score in the maladaptive box. It is equally important that you do not rely on only one mechanism, as circumstances may prevent this being feasible at a time when your stress levels are extremely high. For example, you may depend heavily on social support and find yourself stressed when away on a business trip, or similarly your dependence on leisure activities would be impossible in times of physical injury.

What we all need to do is to become proficient in a variety of stress management skills. Firstly we will look at some activities that will assist in the long term and then move on to look at stress management techniques.

Keeping a stress diary ■

Once you have accepted that you are anxious and are experiencing some of the signs of high stress levels, you are well on the road to recovery. The 'head in the sand' approach is of no use at all and the sooner the problem is acknowledged, the easier it is to deal with.

Coping is facilitated by a careful analysis of the situation: by defining the problem, obtaining all relevant information and then considering alternative approaches to deal with it. Mind Tools (1996) advocate that one of the most effective ways of determining the cause of your stress is keeping a stress diary. You need to record your activities and feelings at regular stages throughout the day. Make a note of the task you are doing, how efficiently you are working, and your thoughts (which we will look at later). After a stressful event, log what the event was, when and why it occurred and the way in which you handled it.

After a month or so, on analysing the data, you should be able to recognize who or what causes you most anxiety and which of your coping strategies worked. There will be occasions when your coping skills were not developed sufficiently or were not appropriate. We now need to turn to some skill development training that may help.

Become change-skilled ■

The mere process of talking to somebody else about the problem bothering the individual reduces many stress symptoms. Talking about the problem with a sympathetic listener is a good start toward dissipating stress. However, stress management requires more. It involves changing something in your lifestyle and since change is the prime cause of stress, we must learn to become change-skilled before we can even consider changing our way of life. Flexibility is the key to effective coping and the greater the range of strategies an individual can call on, the more likely it is that the coping will prove effective.

We are currently in the throes of a huge information revolution and, as with the Industrial Revolution, those of us who resist change will be crushed by it. People who welcome change will be able to exploit the new opportunities opening up on a regular basis. Our success depends on adaptation to, or anticipation of, change.

If we have analysed our situation and identified the factors causing our distress, the obvious next stage is to make changes to our lifestyle that will remove the stressors. If this cannot be achieved we need to learn ways of reducing the impact of the stressors. This, however, is not as easy as it sounds as many of us cannot make changes, and if you cannot make small changes in your life, you have no chance of changing your lifestyle. Can you adapt to small changes? Try keeping your car keys in a different place for one week, or even sleeping on the other side of the bed. If you cannot adjust to these minor changes, you are not ready to tackle the bigger issue.

Even if we can make changes we still need to learn when to make them and when to let situations remain. When we are in danger of suffering high stress, for whatever reason, we must aim to minimize the disturbance to our lifestyles. If, for example, we are going through a divorce or have recently suffered the death of a close relative or friend, it is not the time to consider moving house. We must learn to make the fewest and smallest changes when most stressed. Remember:

- you cannot eliminate change from your life;
- you must learn when to tackle the change and when to let it go; and
- the value you place on what isn't right is what causes stress.

Adopting a healthy lifestyle

Most of us only pay any real attention to our health when we are ill. Clearly, if we took a proactive stance, the improvement in our general health would be likely to improve our immune system sufficiently for us to avoid some of the headaches, coughs and colds we suffer. What must be remembered is that it is not sensible to wait until we are highly stressed before changing our lifestyles. Aside from the fact that this would be the most difficult time to make any changes, we have already seen that our immune systems would already be at a low level.

To be a good stress manager you must be fit and healthy. It is essential that you maintain the strength and stamina needed to meet daily challenges and in order to do this you should:

- eat a balanced diet;
- exercise on a regular basis;
- get regular hours of sleep; and
- have some leisure time – enjoy life.

Eating healthily

We have already seen that stress often influences our eating habits – some people react by over eating, which can lead to weight gain, and which can itself be stressful, while others under eat, which reduces concentration and can make them less responsive to stressful situations.

What we eat is also instrumental in changing our stress levels. The chemicals we consume can cause a surprising amount of the stress we may experience on a daily basis. By eating or drinking certain things we can actually put our bodies under chemical stress.

Similarly, if we are eating an unbalanced diet we may be stressing our bodies by depriving them of essential nutrients. Eating too much for a long period causes obesity. This puts your heart and lungs under stress, overloads your organs and reduces stamina. Indeed, some of the comforts we turn to when stressed actually increase our stress levels.

- *Caffeine*   This is a stimulant, which is consumed in large quantities. It can speed up your system for approximately 18 hours. It is a drug that you can become addicted to and when trying to cut down on your intake you may experience headaches and a rapid pulse.
- *Sugar*   In the short term sugar will boost your energy level but this will soon be replaced by an energy shortage. This is caused by the insulin (which is released by the body to counteract the amount of sugar in your blood stream) continuing to act after the level of blood sugar has normalized.
- *Nicotine*   Cigarettes can, in the very short term, help relaxation but the chemicals inhaled into the body act as a stimulant and its toxic effects increase the heart rate. Additionally, blood pressure and hormone levels increase causing distress.
- *Alcohol and drugs*   Both of these are extremely harmful to the body and can cause serious irreversible damage. In the long term such 'props' disrupt sleep patterns and make the individual drug dependent.

The effects of any of the above are short-lived and do not help in any way to solve the problem responsible for our stress. The way forward is to eat a balanced diet. You can obtain reliable information on dietary needs from your doctor. If you follow those guidelines your body will receive all of the nutrients it requires to function effectively.

Regular exercise

The benefits of regular exercise are immense and I cannot emphasize enough just how important exercise is when trying to manage stress. It is a fact that we now live in an age where nearly all physical activity can and has been replaced by technology. Most large department stores have lifts and escalators to save us walking and we now even feel resentment at having to change the television channel manually if we cannot find the remote control. We appear to be a generation who travel by car everywhere (even to local shops which are a ten minute walk away), use machines to do all of our chores and then pay to visit gymnasiums to exercise! We must learn to timetable exercise into our lives as it not only improves our physical and mental health but also helps to relax tense muscles that in turn helps us to sleep.

There are numerous benefits to be gained from exercise. The physiological changes that occur make a positive contribution in reducing our stress levels. For instance, all exercise increases our blood circulation and this improved flow of blood to the brain provides additional supplies of oxygen and sugars, which are essential in helping us to function properly when stressed. The increased blood flow also facilitates the speedy removal of waste products that build up as a result of the more intense function of the neurones in the brain when an individual is stressed. The build up of toxins, in the short term, can cause unclear thinking, and in the long term can actually cause damage to the brain. The improved circulatory system means that the waste is eliminated efficiently regardless of whether you are exercising; that is, the benefit is permanent providing you keep exercising. Another positive benefit of exercise is the release of chemicals called endomorphins, which result in a general feeling of well-being.

It is important that you select an exercise that you enjoy: if you do not enjoy it, then you will probably not keep doing it. Before contemplating any exercise programme it is important to consider several factors:

- What is your current fitness level? It is of extreme importance that you consult your doctor before starting any rigorous exercise regime, as you could do more harm than good.
- What activities do you enjoy? It is no good deciding to visit the gymnasium every day if you do not enjoy the visits. Such activity will simply add to your stress.
- Are you well coordinated? Which sport best suits your skills?
- How much time do you have available? Some activities will necessitate travelling, for example visits to a public swimming baths or to squash courts. Do you have sufficient time to make such visits on a regular basis?
- Do you need to find an equally enthusiastic partner for the sport? It can be most frustrating if you decide to play a racquet sport and cannot find an opponent at the times suitable to you.

Rest and leisure

A healthy lifestyle will include regular periods of rest, sleep and leisure activities. When we are stressed and there are not enough hours in the day to complete all tasks, we typically abandon all leisure and rest periods and reduce our hours of sleep in an attempt to 'make' time. In the very short term this might be effective, but it soon leads to a tired mind that cannot concentrate and that is totally inefficient. It is, therefore, essential that we maintain our leisure time and ensure that we get the optimum amount of sleep. This will clearly be different for each of us but on average is between seven and eight hours daily.

Enjoy your leisure time

The simple expedient of learning to 'have fun' is an important method of reducing the tensions brought about by stress. Most of us feel guilty if we take breaks or set aside time for hobbies or leisure activities, but it is important to remember that learning to concentrate on a meaningful activity for 30 minutes or more will enable the individual to focus on what they enjoy and forget their problems. This affords the body a respite from the release of the stress chemicals that perpetuate the stress cycle. You should be spending time regularly doing things you enjoy, and remember working hard does not equate with working long hours.

Before reading any further consider whether you have a balanced lifestyle. If you do not seem to have time for anything other than work, there is something wrong with your life, and your health will eventually suffer. It could even result in premature death before you have time to enjoy your well earned retirement.

Adopting the right attitude

Relationships with other people can be either very satisfying or very stressful and unpleasant. While a certain amount of this comes down to their personalities, your attitude has a surprisingly large effect on the way that other people respond to you.

Mind Tools (1996) suggest that when dealing with others it is important to understand the difference between managing people and exploiting them. When you manage a relationship you are improving it for mutual advantage. When you exploit a relationship you are improving your results at the expense of the other person and this behaviour will probably result in your getting a reputation for being selfish and thus make future working relationships even more difficult.

Assertiveness is a skill that is not often well developed but it often produces an early, significant decrease in stress levels. When you deal with other people, you should confidently project your right to have your views taken into consideration. This does not mean aggressively insisting on getting your own way, which irritates other people and tramples on their rights. If you are not assertive then you will probably not be noticed, your triumphs will not be given their due weight and your needs will not be given proper attention. Assertive behaviour does not mean being aggressive, but it does mean that you are entitled to your own opinion and have the right to be listened to and have your views taken seriously. It also means that you can admit to 'not understanding' or 'not knowing' without embarrassment and that you can say 'no' to anyone who asks you to help them without feeling guilty. Generally, assertiveness means that you can behave in a way that you feel is correct and appropriate and not modify that behaviour purely to comply with the views of others.

Another extremely powerful technique when dealing with other people is to try to understand the way they think. Try to think yourself inside their mind. See life through their eyes, feel what they feel and understand their background, influences and motivations. When a colleague says something that you find hurtful or offensive your attitude will often determine the amount of stress you experience. For example, if someone deliberately insults you, you must realize that this is probably caused by a fault of their character. It is very probable that they are irritating and offensive to many other people as well. Examine their comments rationally. If they are unfair, reject them. If rude comments are fair, however upsetting they may be, learn from them.

It is also important that you learn to forgive; this is for you, not the other person. It is pointless bottling up all of your hurt and anger by bearing a grudge. You will lose sleep but the other person will carry on as normal. Forgiving, remember, is not the same as forgetting. Learn from the lesson. You may never trust the other person again or avoid being in their company but make sure you do not use up any more of your energy worrying or fretting about the incident. Why give them even more of your time?

Thought awareness

Stress is in the mind of the beholder

Professor Theo Comperriolle

We can now make use of the stress diaries, where you noted, among other things, your thoughts when stressed. Thought awareness is the process by which you observe your thoughts for a time, and become aware of what is going through your head. Do not try to suppress any thoughts. Just let them run their course while you observe them. After you have kept a stress dairy for several weeks, analyse the data collected and look for negative thoughts, such as having a preoccupation with illness or worrying about your future performance at work and general feelings of inadequacy.

Once you recognize a propensity to negative thinking you can take action to adopt a positive thought process. Positive thinking will not, however, be a solution to everything and needs to be used with common sense. No amount of positive thinking will make everyone who applies it a world class squash player (but a world class squash player is unlikely to have reached this level without being pretty good at positive thinking). Firstly, decide rationally what goals you can realistically attain with hard work, and then use positive thinking to reinforce these. We will look at this in more detail with goal setting and time management.

Imagery (autogenic therapy)

As the name suggests this is a self-produced method of relaxation. This method depends on the development of an association between thoughts and body state. In other words, it is the brain that has to do the work while the rest of the body remains passive. Most of us find particular environments to be very relaxing while others, we know, will cause us to feel anxious and uncomfortable. The principle behind the use of imagery in stress management is that you can train your imagination to place you in a setting that is very relaxing and one in which you are most comfortable. The more practised you become at this, the stronger the experiences will be and the more effective in reducing your stress.

Our senses convert signals from our environment into nerve impulses, which, in turn, feed into areas of the brain that are responsible for interpreting that environment. Imagery, therefore, aims to create a similar set of nerve impulses by simply thinking of an appropriate environment and not actually having to be in that situation. Most of us will be able to master basic autogenics but in order to experience maximum benefits from the more advanced procedures, professional guidance is recommended.

Let us try a simple exercise. Once you are in a comfortable position in a quiet room, imagine a scene that you remember as being very restful and where you were happiest. Try to use all of your senses. Perhaps you are thinking about a holiday scene where you are lying on a beach. Try to visualize the cliffs, sea and sand around you; 'hear' the waves crashing against craggy rocks. Are you able to smell the sea air and feel the warmth of the sun and gentle breeze on your body? Clearly if you do not like the sea, focus on a different scenario such as a country scene, a special occasion or whatever. You will be able to come up with the most effective images for yourself.

Other uses of imagery in relaxation involve mental pictures of stress flowing out of the body, or of stress, distractions and everyday concerns being folded and locked away in a padlocked chest.

Imagery in preparation and rehearsal

This technique can also be used before a big event, allowing you to run through it in your mind. It allows you to practise in advance for anything unusual that might occur, so that you are prepared and already practised in handling it. Imagery also allows you to pre-experience achievement of your goals. This helps to give you the self-confidence you need to do something well.

Learning to relax

Relaxation techniques are particularly effective where high stress levels are caused by the body's physiological reaction to a situation, such as adrenaline release, tense muscles. Deep breathing is a core component of most of these techniques, and it is important that you master diaphragmatic breathing, as this allows the lungs to fill and empty with the minimum of effort. Follow the steps carefully and practise the process frequently until it becomes the 'norm'.

1 Place one hand on your upper chest and one on your abdomen just below your breastbone. Now try to breathe so only your lower hand is moving.
2 Place both hands on the abdomen below the ribs. Breathe in through your nose, allowing your abdomen to rise as your diaphragm moves down.
3 Count to three and then breathe out slowly through your nose. Let out as much air as possible. You should be able to feel your abdomen fall as your diaphragm relaxes.
4 Repeat step 3 four times. Concentrate only on your breathing and expel all other thoughts. You will know if you are doing this correctly as your chest will remain quite still as your abdomen will be doing the work.

Progressive muscular relaxation (PMR)

In order to control stress, which we have defined as 'pulling tight', we need to develop techniques that will 'make loose'. This is the aim of all relaxation techniques. Progressive relaxation involves the individual relaxing various muscle groups in turn. This method also teaches the individual to recognize the feeling of muscles when they are tightening, thus enabling them to begin the exercises as soon as the stress levels rise.

You can apply PMR to any of the muscle groups in your body. Before trying to relax the entire body, experience the sensation of deep relaxation in your hand muscles. Form a fist and now clench your ƒhand as tightly as you can and hold this for a few seconds. Relax your hand to its previous state and then consciously relax it again so that it is as loose as possible. You should be able to feel deep relaxation in the muscles. Don't worry if you can't; keep practising until you achieve this sensation.

You are now ready to try this muscular relaxation procedure on all your muscle groups.

1 Make sure you are comfortable. Wear loose clothes and lie on a mat or blanket with your arms by your sides and feet apart. Use a pillow or cushion to support your head if you need to.
2 Now close your eyes and concentrate on your breathing.
3 Begin by tensing the muscles in your feet. Hold for 5 seconds and then release.
4 Next, tense and release the calf, thigh, buttock and stomach muscles in turn.
5 Clench and release your fists and then all arm muscles.
6 Lift your shoulders up to your ears, hold for 5 seconds and lower. Repeat four times.
7 Rock your head gently from side to side.
8 Yawn and relax.
9 Now you need to work on the facial muscles. Frown and release. Raise and lower your eyebrows. Pucker your mouth and then release.
10 Focus on your breathing and imagine being somewhere safe and warm.
11 Wriggle your fingers and toes and gently move your arms and legs.
12 Roll on to one side and relax for 2 minutes before getting up slowly.

Autogenic training is a natural progression after progressive relaxation and it is practised by concentrating on different phrases suggesting autonomic relaxation. The technique, developed in the 1930s, is designed to promote and give support to the self-regulating systems of the body. These systems automatically regulate important bodily functions such as heart beat and circulation which enable you to relax when not faced with danger. It cannot be stressed enough that whatever relaxation technique you select, it is of paramount importance that it is appropriate to the situation; for example, do not try to reach a state of relaxation while driving, and so on.

Correct breathing

Central to many of the recognized relaxation techniques is mastering the skills of correct breathing. During breathing air is drawn into the lungs where it fills tiny air sacs, which are surrounded by a network of blood vessels. The blood then absorbs the oxygen and transports it to every cell. As the oxygen is absorbed the blood passes carbon dioxide and waste products that are released from the cells back into the air. Exhalation is the most important part of breathing.

If the process is shallow, the cells of the brain and nervous system are affected. This can then affect digestion, complexion and circulation, causing stress, depression and fatigue, and makes stress much harder to deal with. Poor breathing devitalizes your life, and affects your health, posture and flexibility.

Breathing is the link to the inner and outer worlds. It is regulated by the brain and it adjusts to every change of activity or emotion the body goes through. When you breath, you are using one of two patterns; chest or thoracic breathing, and abdominal or diaphragm breathing. Chest breathing is often associated with anxiety or emotional distress. It is also common in people who lead sedentary or stressful lives. Abdominal breathing is the natural breathing of newborn babies and sleeping adults. Inhaled air is drawn deep into the lungs and exhaled as the diaphragm contracts and expands.

Breathing exercises are helpful in reducing generalized anxiety, disorders, panic attacks, agoraphobia, depression, irritability, muscle tension, headaches and fatigue. One extremely popular relaxation method that is based entirely on controlled breathing is yoga. Yoga, which means union, begins with ethical teachings to restrain from antisocial behaviour and ensure positive conduct. The teaching then concentrates on body posture, breathing exercises and the withdrawal of the senses. This helps to gain control of the body and then meditation, contemplation and isolation then help to gain control of the mind (Rice 1992). Research has shown that yogis, who are experts in the practice of yoga, can control their heart processes by muscular control and breathing.

Yoga is renowned for its numerous benefits, but one of the most significant is the role it plays in stress management and reduction.

There are several yoga techniques that can be used to alleviate stress in life as well as to rejuvenate the body, mind and spirit. Contrary to popular belief, you do not have to practise an hour of yoga each day to attain results. In fact, just taking 10–15 minutes out of your schedule can prove to be extremely refreshing and helpful. This is especially beneficial to busy people who often find themselves pressed for time. Yoga's several benefits can be seen by first examining the effects of stress on the body and mind, and then describing the breathing exercises and postures that can be used to overcome stress.

When we are confronted with stressful situations, our mind shifts towards the situation and away from the body's natural balanced state. Breathing becomes rapid and short, while normal breathing is overlooked. This causes a deficiency of oxygen, which is needed to maintain general health, as well as to balance our emotional and mental states. This results in muscular tension, causing increased irritability and anxiousness. There are various breathing exercises and postures that can be used to relieve built-up tension and stress.

Breathing is something we all do, but practising it correctly and consciously is entirely another matter. Practising controlled yogic breathing, or poranayama, is a very valuable technique that will lead to a better and healthier lifestyle. There are several breathing techniques that can be used to relax your body and mind. Some of these include simple breathing, alternate nostril breathing, and complete breathing. These techniques will improve oxygen intake and circulation, thereby relaxing both the mind and body.

Simple breathing is a great technique to start with because it is the basis of all the other breathing techniques. In simple breathing you take the time to observe your natural breathing because this allows you to become more aware of your breath. Increased awareness of your breathing leads to your peace of mind and purifies all the breathing channels. It also allows you to be more alert and relaxed in stressful situations. Doing just one or two minutes of this simple breathing will make you more relaxed and will alleviate some of the stress you encounter each day. Alternate nostril breathing can be used to attain tranquillity and to have peace of mind. After practising a couple of rounds of this, your breathing will naturally get deeper and smoother, thereby improving the quality of blood circulating to all areas of the body. Complete breathing is also very beneficial as it revitalizes your energy and quickly relaxes the entire body. Practising postures with steady relaxed breathing can also alleviate the physical effects of stress and accumulated tension. Some quick, but effective yoga exercises that can be practised are neck movements and shoulder socket rotations, which relax the neck and upper back, and several stretches can improve circulation. Having good circulation is extremely important because our life fluids are blood and oxygen. By encouraging a good supply of both it revitalizes the body and allows you to be more focused and concentrate clearly.

Other factors that cause stress are suppressing emotions and worrying needlessly. Instead of suppressing your feelings, try to gain a better understanding of them by meditating and focusing on your breath. It is also crucial to understand that worrying about the future does not produce a favourable outcome and in fact detracts from your performance. Worrying causes a shortness of breath, creating stress and tension, which are both harmful to your mind as well as body. It is important to focus on the present moment, using it to plan the future and to do what you can, to the best of your ability.

Another method of relaxation training is meditation. We meditate for a variety of reasons: stress relief; increased focus and creativity; relaxation; and improved health and well-being. Meditation is among the most popular 'alternative' therapies, and has proved to be so effective that it is now being used as a natural and holistic response to stress and illness in mainstream hospitals and corporate offices throughout the USA. Science has shown that meditation balances the hemispheres of the brain, resulting in improved brain function and increased levels of neurochemical opiates, which are the 'feel good' chemicals within the brain. These natural opiates act as mood enhancers, reducing stress and delivering the natural high of life with no undesirable side effects. This balanced condition is experienced by the mediator as the peaceful, blissful, opiated state of awareness that results from the release of significant levels of neurochemicals.

From a contemporary scientific perspective, meditation produces certain measurable effects within the human brain. Based on this research, we now understand that the mediator's journey involves the actual alteration of the electrical activity within the human brain. The studies reveal that brain wave frequencies progressively decelerate. Balance, or synchronization, of the two sides of the brain increases over time and there is an increase in the production of neurochemical endorphins. The result is the gradual development of whole brain function through hemispheric balance.

Values and goal planning

It has been shown that we are goal-directed creatures, who strive for meaning, significance and purpose. Since a lack of achievable goals results in stress and anxiety it is not surprising that most successful people have at least one factor in common: they all set themselves goals and work towards them. Researchers into survivors of stressful environments have concluded that those best equipped to survive in places such as concentration camps were those who had or created goals and had something to aim for.

Before we can set goals, we have to determine what we want to change in our lives. Ask yourself the following questions.

- What do you want to spend your energy on?
- What do you value the most between work, home and health?
- Which of these do you spend most of your energy on each day?

I expect most of you answered that you want to spend your energy on your friends and family, doing things that you enjoy, and that you value your health greatly. I doubt, however, if your answer to the third question reflected those wishes. Furthermore, if I now ask you how much time you devote to looking after your health compared to the hours afforded to your work, I suspect the answer would be 'not much'.

Do you eat balanced meals and take regular exercise? I doubt that many of us do, and yet we still maintain that we value our health. (Most people certainly value their health when they are ill!) It is, therefore, essential that we stop paying lip service to what we say we value and start planning our lives in order to achieve our aims. Decide on what you want to achieve in six months' time and break it down into monthly and weekly targets. Write it down and place the list somewhere where you will see it several times a day. As previously discussed, when we are not in control of our lives, our stress levels rise. Just the feeling of not being able to schedule simple things, such as the time of day your furniture will be delivered, causes most of us anxiety and we pace the floor, keeping a close watch outside the front door for the delivery van to arrive. There are times, however, when the only difference between keeping control and losing control comes down to planning our time carefully. If we plan well we can often anticipate or avoid potential problems. Rice (1992) suggest that even under such stressful conditions, professionals who have established their priorities and organized their lives will continue to function efficiently.

This planning process should also include the setting of self-improvements goals. These could take the form of further qualifications to be gained or improving self-image. It is also possible to plan for stressful occasions. By anticipating stress you can prepare for it and work out how to control it when it happens. To reduce the problem usually means taking control of the situation. Let us consider the case of a lecturer who is worried about delivering a lecture to a group of students while being assessed by a senior colleague.

Although the lecturer cannot remove the cause, they can increase control of the situation by preparing well, checking that the overhead projector works in advance and ensuring that the appropriate administrative work, such as registers, schemes of work and so on, are readily available. Cognitive redefinition is also an effective mechanism in reducing the problem. An individual needs to change the way they view the situation. In our example, the lecturer may rationalize and decide that once the lecture is prepared there shouldn't be any real problems; it is what they do every day of the week and there are never any problems.

Goal planning

Once you have completed the stress inventory grids and the other questionnaires, you will have more insight into yourself and your susceptibility to stress. The next stage is to set about doing something to improve the situation. Set yourself realistic goals. There is no way that a harassed over-worked individual is going to become an easy going, 'laid-back' type overnight. You are looking for improvements; not miracles. Any improvement that is to be long lasting and worthwhile must be achieved gradually. The habits of a lifetime are not going to be set aside in an instant, but there is no reason why you cannot start *now*.

Although you may not be able to eradicate some of your problems, it should certainly be possible to ease each situation, or control how much stress that situation causes you. The best approach is to treat the whole matter as you would any work problem that may arise. First of all you have to identify the nature of the problem: perform a work stress inventory. Now you must decide on a possible solution. For example, if your stress is caused by travelling, it might be worth starting work a little earlier or finishing a little later, thereby avoiding the traffic jams as much as possible.

Seven steps in goal planning

1 Decide what you really want to achieve. What are your goals?
2 Once you have generated this list of goals, look at your goals closely to make sure that they are achievable. You may find incompatibilities such as a wish to gain further qualifications and a wish to spend more time with your family. You will need to eliminate one of these goals or modify both of them.

3 Write out your modified goals in terms of clear aims; for example, 'by next academic year I will have written and had typed the first three chapters of my PhD thesis'.

4 Write an action plan or a series of specific activities for the accomplishment of that goal. For example, for completing your PhD, activities might be:

- buy computer/computer software package;
- enrol on research methodology course;
- buy a book on statistical analysis;
- set aside Monday, Wednesday and Friday evenings for research work;
- arrange to meet your tutor and show them the first draft before the end of 2000; and
- set up a proper study at home.

5 Identify potential problems and make plans to overcome them. For example, if the foreseen problem is that you might have to work late two evenings each week you may wish to decide to work on your PhD for eight hours on Sundays instead of the two evenings.

6 Work out a reward system; for example, 'If I've completed the data collection by September I will treat myself to a five day shopping trip to London'.

7 Try to keep the end result in mind as it will help to motivate you to reach your goal.

(Adapted from Powell 1992)

Time management

Most of us are guilty of regularly thinking 'There are never enough hours in the day', or 'I wish it was time to go home'. A lot of our stress is caused by trying to do too much, or by wishing time away. We know that there are, and always will be, 24 hours in the day and only seven days in the week, and yet we continually fight to control time. This is clearly a battle we can never win and it would, therefore, be far more sensible to put our efforts into learning how to manage our time. We cannot change the number of hours in the day, so we need to change the way in which we spend the hours. What changes can you make that would allow you to do the things that you enjoy? This gives us an opportunity to recharge our batteries. As children we played; sadly, as adults, we feel guilty if we spend time on fun and leisure. In order to find this time we need to organize ourselves.

- What *must* you do?
- What *should* you do?
- What can you *leave*?

Time management is really only a term used to describe time that is used in the most effective and productive way possible (Mind Tools 1996). It helps you to reduce the level of your occupational stress by training you in the skills needed to be more in control of your time and helping you to become more productive. Clearly there are many benefits from this, not least being that you will have more 'free' time to relax and enjoy your hobbies and leisure activities.

Where to begin

- Break up overwhelming tasks into smaller jobs. Set deadlines for completing the entire task and work on it a little bit every day.
- Draw up a 'to do' list of all the tasks you need to complete in the short term (within the next week), the mid term (the next month) and the long term. Then each day draw up a list of things that you need to do today. Regularly review your 'to do' lists and prioritize each task in terms of its urgency and importance. I find it helps to have a list of smaller tasks that I can tick off as and when they are completed. This way I can see that I am making progress.
- When planning your work schedule, attempt to balance routine tasks with the more enjoyable jobs. If possible, it is a good idea to begin the day with an enjoyable job or at least one that isn't likely to cause stress, then the sense of achievement will set you in a positive frame of mind for the rest of the day.
- Combat paper shuffling by endeavouring to handle each piece of paper only once. Read it, act upon it, file it or throw it away.
- Clear the top of your desk and put everything out of sight except for the task you are currently working on.
- Identify your prime time for working, when your energy levels are high, and use it for the complex tasks; save the trivial task for non prime time. Most people tend to be either larks (at their best in the morning) or night owls (at their best in the late afternoon).
- Try to batch phone calls or trivial or routine tasks and tackle them as one task.
- When making an appointment in your diary, enter a finishing time as well as a start time. Allocate time exclusively to yourself, to enable you to think, to plan and write up urgent reports.

Some general advice ■

Begin by looking at the cause of your stress.

- Does your stress rise because your expectations are not met? Reappraise and establish goals.
- Do you know that a particular occasion will be stressful? Anticipating coping is needed – prepare, plan and rehearse. This will increase your confidence.
- Is there a particular time when you feel overloaded? Use time management, prioritize and delegate.
- Is the stress due to an increase of adrenaline? Use relaxation techniques, which will slow the release of the chemical.
- Is the stress due to relationships or specific events? Use thought awareness and imagery.
- Is the stress long term? Change your lifestyle.

Just remember Ralph Waldo Emerson's words: 'If you always do what you have always done, you will always get what you always got'. Remember, you are responsible for your stress level. Recognizing the signs and symptoms you experience when your stress level is rising is the first step to coping. Become stress-skilled. Identify the situations you find difficult to handle and experiment with the different coping strategies until you find one that suits your needs. Finally, stop worrying – it may never happen.

Why worry?

There are only two things to worry about,
Either you are well or you are sick.
If you are well, then there is nothing to worry about,
But if you are sick there are two things to worry about:
Either you get well or you will die.
If you get well there is nothing to worry about.
If you die there are only two things to worry about:
Either you will go to heaven or to hell.
If you go to heaven there is nothing to worry about,
But if you go to hell,
You will be so damn busy shaking hands with your friends
You won't have time to worry.

Anon

The individual's ten commandments for effective stress management

1 Thou shalt recognize your strengths and weaknesses and accept yourself as you are.
2 Thou shalt eat a healthy diet, making sure you intake all of the essential nutrients and not poison yourself with chemicals/drugs/ alcohol.
3 Thou shalt take regular exercise as part of a healthy living programme.
4 Thou shalt rest regularly. Try to ensure you get seven hours' sleep every night and that you rest for short intervals throughout the day.
5 Thou shalt relax, by doing the things that take your mind off your problems. Concentrate on positive thoughts.
6 Thou shalt enjoy life. Do the things you like doing. Take up hobbies and interests.
7 Thou shalt be flexible and accept change as a part of life. Stop trying to swim against the tide.
8 Thou shalt set aside realistic goals and accept that some things cannot be achieved.
9 Thou shalt organize your life. Manage your time more effectively and make sure you afford most available time to what you value most.
10 Thou shalt know yourself. Learn to recognize the signs and symptoms of your distress and take appropriate action.

You must always remember that you have to take responsibility for your own health and therefore it is imperative that you take action as soon as you begin to feel anxious or stressed. If you are fortunate, you will also have the support of your organization to help you deal with the problem. In Chapter 7 I will look at some of the ways in which management can improve the well-being of their workforce.

7

ORGANIZATIONS AND STRESS MANAGEMENT

The success of any organization will, ultimately, depend on its human resource. It is therefore logically and economically sound for management to invest in approaches that enhance the health of their employees and keep the level of occupational stress at its optimum level. There will, naturally, be occasions where an organization is more stressful than usual. Having a fit and relaxed workforce will ensure that the crisis is met with calm competence and without a disastrous aftermath. It is at these times that you realize that the action you have taken to help with stress management is really cost-effective.

One of the problems facing organizations is that stress is not an easily defined concept and therefore its symptoms are not quickly recognized. In his opening speech at the TUC Conference 'Stress: Who is Liable?', Frank Davies, Chairman of the Health and Safety Commission (HSC) stated:

> We find stress a difficult subject to talk about because there are probably as many definitions of it as there are psychologists. The HSC says that stress is the reaction people have to excessive pressures or other types of demand placed on them and they feel they cannot cope. Pressure at work is not intrinsically bad, but when it gets too much we undergo the reaction we call stress and this can show itself through physical and behavioural symptoms.

The HSE's 1990 *Survey of Self-reported Stress-related Illness in England and Wales* suggests that approximately 7500 employees were absent from work because of the manifestations of stress and that such action costs British industry in excess of £100 million every year. It is surprising, therefore, that up until the 1990s very few organizations were involved in the development of stress management programmes. This could have been due to ignorance of how to deal with the problem, a lack of organizational interest or, as some managers liked to think, there was no stress in their organizations.

Although there is no specific Act of Parliament that controls stress in the workplace in the UK, an employer is responsible for the health, safety and welfare of their employees. The 1992 Management of Health and Safety at Work (MHSW) Regulations charge all employers with the duty of: 'Making a suitable and sufficient assessment of the risks to which they are exposed whilst they are at work . . . for the purpose of identifying the measure he needs to take' (MHSW Regulations 1992: s.3). Today further changes in employment law have forced even the most reluctant manager to address the issue. Employers have a duty of care to their employees, covering both their physical and mental well-being. In 1996 the High Court pronounced: 'they must not cause them psychiatric damage by the volume or character of work they are required to perform'.

Possibly as a direct result of this pronouncement, the consequences of the neglect of employee welfare can now be felt by the organizations concerned in the form of litigation, and since the pronouncement many such cases have been reported by the media. In 1996, for example, Mr John Walker was awarded £175,000 in damages against Northumberland County Council. The importance of *Walker v Northumberland County Council* (1995) is that it was the first case in legal history where an employee was awarded compensation for psychiatric damage suffered as a result of occupational stress. In the judgement of this case, it was stated that: 'Whereas the law on the extent of this duty has developed almost exclusively in cases involving physical injury to the employee as distinct from injury to his mental health, there is no logical reason why risk of psychiatric damage should be excluded from the scope of the duty of care'. One year later there were 400 similar cases waiting to go before the courts.

In future, all employers will be well advised to have a stress management policy and a stress management programme in place to avoid the risk of damages being sought against them by their employees. In addition to reducing the probability of litigation, organizations who have introduced such policies and programmes will be more likely to enjoy a reduced level of absenteeism, increased productivity, lower staff turnover rates and improved morale and motivation.

A logical approach for an employer to take is the thorough assessment of the work place to determine the nature and extent of the risk of work-related stress occurring. This is a standard risk-management approach that applies to any hazard. Control measures are then implemented on the basis of the assessment findings.

There is no legal duty on employers to address stress arising outside work due to circumstances such as financial difficulties or relationship breakdown. However, as the differences between work and personal matters are sometimes blurred and work is often affected by stress outside the work place, it is usually in the employer's interest to deal sympathetically with stressed employees no matter where the causes lie. Professor Compernolle (1997) suggests that a person's resilience is a combination of the individual's support system (support they receive from colleagues and management at work and from family and friends at home), their fitness level and the way in which they appraise situations. Although the culture of the organization will largely determine the degree of support afforded to the personnel, management must be aware that any actions they take that undermine their employees' domestic and social arrangements (such as sending staff away on residential training courses) will have the effect of reducing their levels of support and are therefore likely to increase their stress levels.

Providing an independent employee advisory and referral service is a popular and cost effective strategy adopted by some employers.

Recognize the signs ▪

Individuals should be aware of stress and be able to recognize the signs that their stress levels are too high, but managers too should be able to identify stress-related problems in the work place.

Worksafe, Western Australia (WWA) recommends that organizations should look for tell-tale signs that problems or situations are causing high stress levels. Their report suggests that the following four areas may indicate a stress problem in your organization. However, they are only valid if they follow a period when no such signs were evident.

Performance at work

- There is a distinct decline in output or productivity with no clear reason.
- Error rates increase and there is excessive wastage.
- Workflow and planning deteriorate.
- Deadlines are not met.
- The standard of decision making becomes poor or non-existent.

Employee morale

- Motivation decreases and commitment to the organization declines.
- An increase in time at work does not lead to improved results.
- Internal sabotage may occur.

Relationships at work

- A team spirit is difficult to maintain.
- Tension between colleagues increases and decisions become harder to reach.
- There is a demand for more precise instructions.
- Industrial relations deteriorate.

Sickness absenteeism

- Vague illnesses increase.
- Breaks from work increase.
- Late arrival and early departure becomes more frequent.

Although this list is not definitive it does enable stress problems to be detected at an early stage. Managers then need to look at the action they need to take to improve the situation.

Approaches to the problem ■

One of the more obvious ways in which an organization can help reduce the level of occupational stress among its workforce is to promote the health and fitness of its employees; after all, we have already advised that each person should adopt a healthy lifestyle. It can foster health promotion by: providing sports and exercise facilities or subsidizing membership of health clubs; ensuring that a variety of foods that provide a balanced diet are available in the staff canteen; and, if it has not already done so, introducing a no-smoking campaign. If problems are detected, although there is, unfortunately, no single approach that can be adopted to prevent stress occurring, there are five factors that are generally recognized as being good practice.

Good management

This should include openness and a sincere regard for all employees. There is clearly nothing wrong with informing all staff that they are paid to work and work hard provided there is a consistent approach and all employees are treated fairly, with equity and without harassment. Managers would do well to remember that positive feedback is a great motivator and morale booster when given appropriately.

Many employees do not come to work purely for the financial reward. They also look for stimulation, satisfaction and meaningful social contact. A certain type of management style is therefore crucial in order to retain a productive and interested workforce. Employers need to demonstrate a genuine interest in their workforce and to engender a supportive culture. In order to do this, they should:

- ensure they are accessible to staff to discuss problems and anxieties;
- take a lead in changing the perception that admitting to being stressed is admitting you cannot cope;
- engender team spirit;
- recognize individuals' fears of returning to work after absence and provide support; and
- devise induction and training programmes, not only for new staff but for staff being given new roles (for example how to write documentation).

It is vital that a good two-way communication channel exists in every organization as open and clear communication helps to allay uncertainty.

Good organization

A person's work and occupational stature may play an important role in their sense of identity, self-esteem and psychological well-being. In other words, clear targets must be set with clear policies, plans and recognition for achievement.

A healthy corporate attitude

A healthy and fit workforce is more motivated and productive. Let all employees know that the organization takes fitness seriously and is committed to assisting any employee experiencing difficulties. Take the necessary steps to ensure that no employee feels guilty about being stressed and provide encouragement for them to seek assistance and relief.

Successfully manage change

Commitment to continuous improvement and increased access to information has required organizations to make changes more frequently in order to stay competitive and meet customer needs. Unfortunately people have not yet adjusted to the process of frequent and rapid change and often find the uncertainty of change stressful. The successful management of change includes employee involvement in the decision, the planning and the process of implementing change.

An appropriate management style

Many employees do not come to work only for the income. As previously discussed, they also look for stimulation, satisfaction and meaningful social contact. Employers have benefited considerably from this shift, but it needs a certain management style to retain a productive and interested workforce. Autocratic and bullying tactics are not tolerated. Employers need to demonstrate a genuine interest in their workforce without inconsistency or indifference.

In summary, WWA state that if managers wish to reduce or remove unnecessary stress, they should:

- ensure that the confidence and competence of their employees is not eroded;
- provide a consistent approach in their management style;
- make sure they have good two-way communication;
- provide well defined tasks with clear responsibilities and authority, with adequate relief if the job is excessively monotonous or boring;
- use targets that are challenging but achievable;
- use flexible work schedules that are planned and agreed;
- define their objectives and advertise them widely, being prepared to negotiate adjustments if approached;
- treat people fairly, with equity and without bullying or harassment and ensure that their managers and supervisors do the same; and
- provide positive feedback when appropriate.

Providing assistance

Offering assistance to employees with stress problems works best if you are not seen to be prying into their private lives. If the stress is creating a work problem, deal only with the work problem. If you raise the stress aspect you will inevitably be drawn into causes and, unless you are professionally qualified, you run the risk of making the situation worse.

Access to an independent, qualified employee referral service is a common avenue of assistance in work places. The employer often funds the initial counselling sessions. Employees requiring ongoing or longer-term counselling are referred to other service providers. Around 3–4 per cent of your employees will use the service each year. But a counselling service alone will not assist your organization in the long term. If it is too frequently used it could indicate that your stress prevention strategies are not working. Are you:

- encouraging staff to learn about stress and self-manage their stress levels;
- training line managers to deal with employee problems effectively;
- encouraging a relaxed, efficient and productive work place; and
- using periodic anonymous surveys to obtain employee feedback?

In 1990, the Education Service Admission Committee (ESAC) published a report that recommended that stress problems need to be approached from both the organizational and individual levels with each making an important contribution. The working party set up by the TUC in 1993 concurred with this view and saw occupational stress as a problem that arises from a sick organization and not a sick individual. Those who have conducted research into this subject in the education section have concluded that the way forward must be managements' recognition of the concept of stress in their colleges. Senior staff must acknowledge that there can be a correlation between stress and illness and that it in no way signifies weakness or incompetence.

In June 1999, the Universities and Colleges Employers Association (UCEA) published guidelines to help institutions deal with occupational stress. UCEA states that one of the chief aims of stress intervention is to 'keep people at work, productive and at their optimum performance' (UCEA 1999: 10). There are a number of ways in which management can begin to address stress problems but the main ones are:

- practising good management;
- encouraging group problem solving to discuss perceived stressors and put forward suggestions for appropriate action;
- providing good support systems;
- increasing awareness of stress problems so that they are more easily identified; and
- developing a supportive culture and improving coping techniques.

Each college will need to analyse its own situation and, having considered the leadership styles and culture of the organization, develop its own style of staff support.

It is vital that all staff are involved in developing the stress management policy and programme to avoid further increasing any feelings of isolation and helplessness. Human resource management specialists advocate that group problem solving can aid team development, increase team spirit and encourage the involvement of a supportive culture. Managers must also be heedful of trying to squeeze further meetings into an already hectic day thereby further increasing the lecturers' workloads.

Regardless of how proactive the college and the individual try to be there will still remain instances when some lecturers will have high stress levels. On such occasions, tertiary measures must be implemented to help those individuals recover. Employee Assistance Programmes (EAPs) have significant potential for reducing worker distress. For this potential to be realized, EAPs will need to incorporate a primary prevention component and begin providing feedback to organizations with respect to stressful work environment factors. In light of the sensitivity of worker confidentiality, such feedback will have to be provided in a manner that prevents individual worker identification. Feedback from an EAP in the form of summary statistics would permit organizations to pinpoint high stress departments to establish a starting point for more in-depth stress assessment studies. Providing an independent employee advisory and referral service is a popular and cost-effective strategy adopted by some employers.

Another method used to help staff is counselling. Stress counselling and stress management courses are well established in the USA and are slowly beginning to become more commonplace in the UK. Approximately 150 of the UK's major companies, including the Post Office and Whitbread, currently provide stress counselling for their employees and claim that the service has helped efficiency and staff morale. It is necessary, however, to ensure that it does not lead to a false sense of security that counselling can prevent stress.

The professionals providing the service will listen, help and support the lecturer to develop their own skills and resources, which are essential if they are to deal more effectively with their futures.

The college's ten commandments for effective stress management

1 Thou shalt have commitment at senior level. This is vital for ensuring that resources are made available and agreed action is implemented.
2 Thou shalt recognize stress as a legitimate problem or illness and become instrumental in changing the current perception of stress as weakness and incompetence.
3 Thou shalt involve all staff in determining an appropriate stress-management policy.
4 Thou shalt be proactive rather than reactive.
5 Thou shalt ensure that there are efficient communication channels in the college.
6 Thou shalt acknowledge that stress management is an ongoing task.

7 Thou shalt, with the staff, agree shared objectives.
8 Thou shalt ensure that the college environment is as conducive to work as possible.
9 Thou shalt ensure that appropriate staff development programmes are available for all staff.
10 Thou shalt support any individuals who are experiencing high stress levels.

Whether we begin the journey down the spiral depends on how we view the causes of our problems and how effective we are at managing them. Stress management can help individuals and organizations identify existing and potential personal and corporate stressors and develop more appropriate strategies for the future. Learning to manage stress helps promote individual and organizational well-being in the interests of ourselves and everyone around us.

All reported evidence suggests that lecturers in FE and HE are experiencing high levels of occupational stress, with the most prominent stressors being unsympathetic management, unrealistic targets, lack of support, the inability to influence change, harassment, office politics and job insecurity (Palmer 1994). The problem seems likely to worsen as competitive pressures and the economic climate force more colleges to downsize further, which will result in more pressure being placed on the remaining staff. Indeed, many highly qualified and experienced academics have reported that they would not choose to enter the profession if the clock could be turned back, and others will retire early.

Although a small minority of lecturers will use stress as an excuse for not working very hard, this must not detract from the fact that most academics push themselves too hard and reach a point where their work and health begin to suffer.

We all need to learn to manage our stress levels so that we can continue to produce high quality work over long periods, even when faced with sustained pressure. It is crucial that each person recognizes their own signs and symptoms of stress, learns how to relax and, most importantly, learns how and when to implement stress management strategies. Managers, on the other hand, need to take a pro-active role and implement a support system to alleviate the current stress. They must encourage their academic staff to participate in staff development programmes, which will help them reflect on and discuss stressful events.

It seems very likely that occupational stress will continue to present a major threat to the financial health and efficiency of FE and HE colleges. Increasing health and safety legislation will help to raise public awareness of the problem and hopefully we will witness colleges becoming more proactive. Nevertheless, we owe it to ourselves to ensure that our jobs do not damage our health and we must, there-fore, watch for early signs and symptoms of the illness and act accordingly. This way, we can improve both the quality and quantity (in years) of our lives.

BIBLIOGRAPHY

Abouserie, R. (1996) Stress: coping and job satisfaction in university academic staff, *Educational Psychology*, 16(1): 49–56.

Association of University Teachers (1994) *Long Hours, Little Thanks*. London: AUT.

Bandura, A. (1977) *Social Learning Theory*. Englewood Cliffs, NJ: Prentice Hall.

Bandura, A., Adams, N.E. and Beyer, J. (1977) Cognitive Processes Mediating Behavioural Change, *Journal of Personality and Social Psychology*, 35(3): 125–39.

Bartlett, D. (1998) *Stress – Perspectives and Processes*. Buckingham: Open University Press.

Beels, E., Hopson, B. and Scally, M. (1991) *Assertiveness – A Positive Process*. Chalford, Glos: Mercury Business Books.

Belloc, N.B. and Breslow, L. (1972) Relationship of Physical Health Status and Health Practices, *Preventive Medicine*, 1: 409–21.

Brosschott, J.F., Benschop, R.J., Godaert, G.L.R. *et al.* (1994) Internal, powerful others and change locus of control: relationships with personality, coping, stress and health, *Personality & Individual Differences*, 16(6): 839–52.

Burns, R.B. (1980) *Essential Psychology for Students and Professionals in the Health and Social Services*. Lancaster: MTP Press.

Burns, D.D. (1980) *Feeling Good: The New Mood Theory*. New York: William Morrow.

Butler, G. (1988) *Review of Self-efficacy: The Exercise of Control, British Journal of Clinical Psychology*, 37(4): 470.

Cartwright, S. (1995) Stress management – the challenges of a changing business environment, *Business Studies Magazine*, 8(1): 22–6.

Cartwright, S. and Cooper, C.L. (1997) *Managing Workplace Stress*. Thousand Oaks, CA: Sage Publications.

CBI (1991) *Promoting Mental Health at Work*. London: CBI/DoH.

Collins, S. (1995) Stress and social work lecturers: dreaming spires, ivory towers or besieged in concrete blocks? *Social Work Education*, 14(4): 11–37.

Compernolle, T. (1997) Stress: Friend and Foe, in T. Compernolle. Stress and Workstress Directory. http://web.inter.N1/.net/hcc/T.Compernolle/ strescat.htm

Cooper, C.L. (ed.) (1983) *Stress Research: Issues for the Eighties*. Chichester: John Wiley.

Cooper, C.L. and Marshall, J. (1976) Occupations Sources of Stress: A Review of the Literature Relating to Coronary Heart Disease and Mental Ill Health, *Journal of Occupations Psychology*, 4(9): 11–28.

Cooper, C.L. and Davidson, M.J. (1982) *High Pressure: Working Lives of Women Managers*. London: Fontana.

Cooper, C. and Hingley, P. (1986) *Stress and the Nursing Manager*. London: Harper & Row.

Cooper, C.L. and Payne, R. (eds) (1994) *Causes, Coping and Consequences of Stress at Work*. New York: John Wiley.

Cooper, C.L. and Cartwright, S. (1996) *Mental Health and Stress in the Workplace: A Guide for Employers*. London: HMSO.

Cox, T. (1990) The recognition and measurement of stress: conceptual and methodological issues, in E.N. Corlett and J. Wilson (eds) *Evaluation of Human Work*. London: Taylor and Francis.

Cox, T. (1993) *Stress Research and Stress Management: Putting Theory to Work*. HSE Research Contract. Nottingham: University of Nottingham.

Cox, T. and Mackay, C. (1979) Introductory remarks: occupational stress and the quality of working life, in T. Cox and C. Mackay (eds) *Response to Stress: Occupational Aspects*. Guildford: IPC Science and Technology Press.

Daft, R.L. (1992) *Organization Theory and Design*. St Paul, USA: South Western College Publishing.

Daily Mail (1996) £79bn bill for stress at work. *Daily Mail,* 1 October.

Davies, F. (1997) *Stress – Who is Liable?* TUC conference proceedings. London: TUC.

Day, M. (1994) An interview with Cary Cooper, *Nursing Times*, 90(44): 23.

Dobson, C.B. (1982) *Stress: The Hidden Adversary*. Lancaster: MTP Press.

Doyle, C. and Hind, P. (1989) *Occupational Stress, Burnout and Job Status in Female Academics*. Oxford: Blackwell.

Doyle, C. and Hind, P. (1998) Occupational stress, burnout and job status of female academics, *Gender Work & Organisation*, 5(2): 67–82.

Earley, P. (1994) *Lecturers' Workload and Factors Affecting Stress Levels*. A Research Report. London: NATFHE.

Edwarde, J.E. and Cooper, C.L. (1998) Research in stress, coping and health: theoretical and methodological issues. *Psychological Medicine*, 18: 15–20.

Elliot, G.R. and Eisdorferc, C. (eds) (1982) *Stress and Human Health Analysis and Implications of Research*. A study by the Institute of Medicine, National Academy of Science. New York: Springer.

Ellis, A. (1962) *Reason and Emotion in Psychotherapy*. New York: Struart.

Ellis, A. (1997) *Workplace Bullying*. Oxford: Ruskin College, Oxford.

Employment of Social Affairs, European Community (ESAC) (1990) *Managing Occupational Stress: A Guide for Managers and Teachers in the School Sector*. London: Health and Safety Executive.

Ferris, G.R., Frink, D.D., Galang, M.C. *et al.* (1996) Perceptions of organisational politics: prediction, stress-related implications and outcomes, *Human Relations*, 49(2): 233–67.

Fisher, S. (1994) *Stress in Academic Life – The Mental Assembly Line.* Buckingham: The Society for Research into Higher Education and Open University Press.

Fletcher, B.C. (1988) The epidemiology of occupational stress, in C.L. Cooper and R. Payne (eds) *Causes, Coping and Consequences of Stress at Work.* Chichester: Wiley.

Fotinatos, R. and Cooper, C. (1993) *Occupational Stress Survey.* Manchester: UMIST.

Friedman, H.S. and Booth-Kewley, S. (1987) 'The disease-prone personality': a meta-analytic view of the construct, *American Psychologist*, 42: 539–55.

Gallie, D. and White, M. (1993) *Employee Commitment and the Skills Revolution.* London: Policy Studies Institute.

Gelfand, D.M. (1962) The influence of self-esteem on rate of verbal conditioning and social matching behaviour, *Journal of Abnormal Soc. Psychology*, 65: 259.

Gmelch, W.H., Lovrich, N.P. and Wilke, P.K. (1994) Sources of stress in academe: a national perspective, *Research in Higher Education*, 20(4): 477–90.

Gove, W.R. (1972) The relationship between sex roles, marital status and mental illness, *Journal of Social Forces*, 51(1): 34–44.

Hall, G. (1994) Pressure gauge, *Personnel Today*, May: 29–30.

Handy, C. (1985) *Understanding Organizations.* New York: Penguin.

Hazell, T. (1996) Why stress is breeding the office superbully. *Daily Mail*, 28 November.

Health and Safety Executive (1990) *Survey of Self-reported Stress-related Illness in England and Wales.* London: HMSO.

Health and Safety Executive (1995) *Stress at Work: A Guide for Employers.* London: HMSO.

Health and Safety Executive (1999) *One in Five Stressed at Work – Results of Stress Survey.* Press release E101: 99.

Health and Safety at Work Act (1974). Elizabeth II. Chapter 37. London: HMSO.

Health Education Authority (1988) *Stress in the Public Sector.* London: Health Education Authority.

Hickcox, E.S. (1983) *Administration of an Educational Administration Department.* Toronto: Ontario Institute for Studies in Education.

Holden, R. (1992) *Stress Busters.* London: HarperCollins.

Holmes, T.H. and Rahe, R.H. (1967) The social readjustment rating scale, *Journal of Psychosomatic Research*, 2: 213–18.

Hope, J. (1997) Stress 'as bad for heart as smoking'. *Daily Mail*, 2 December.

Hope, J. (1999) One in four is laid low by stress at work. *Daily Mail*, 21 May.

Hopson, B. and Scally, M. (1984) *Build Your Own Rainbow: A Workbook for Career and Life Management.* Leeds: Lifeskills Associates.

Hopson, B. and Scally, M. (1989) *Time Management: Conquer the Clock.* Leeds: Lifeskills Associates.

Jones, D.M. (1983) Noise, in G.R.J. Hockey (ed.) *Stress and Fatigue in Human Performance.* Chichester: Wiley & Sons.

Koenker, H. (n.d.) Stress and the Immune System. http://www.econ.iuic.edu/~hanko/Bio/stress.html (accessed 8 May 1999).

Kobasa, S. (1979) Stressful life events, personality and health: an inquiry into hardiness, *Journal of Personality and Social Psychology*, 42(1): 168–77.

Kompier, M. and Lennart, L. (1995) *Stress at Work: Causes, Effects and Prevention: A Guide for Small and Medium-sized Enterprises*. London: The Stationery Office.

Lazarus, R.S. (1966) *Psychological Stress in the Coping Process*. New York: McGraw-Hill.

Lazarus, A.A. (1971) *Behaviour Therapy and Beyond*. New York: McGraw-Hill.

Lazenby, J.P. (1989) Occupational stressors and coping strategies: an assessment of Lloyds Bank network managers. Unpublished MSc thesis, University of Glasgow.

Locke, G.A. (1976) The nature and causes of job satisfaction, in M.D. Dunnette (ed.) *Handbook of Industrial and Organisational Psychology*. Skokie, IL: Rand McNally.

Locke, J.H. (1976) Provision of information and advice for the protection of health and safety at work. *ASLIB Proceedings*, January.

Looker, T. and Gregson, O. (1997) *Managing Stress*. London: Hodder & Stoughton.

Management of Health and Safety at Work Regulations (1992), Statutory instruments 1992 2051. London: The Stationery Office.

McKenna, E.F. (1987) *Psychology in Business: Theory and Applications*. London: Psychology Press.

Mangan, P. (1994) A study in overwork, *Nursing Times*, 90(44): 22–3.

Margolis, B.L. and Kroes, W.H. (1974) Work and the health of man, in J. O'Toole (ed.) *Work and the Quality of Life*. Cambridge, MA: MIT Press.

Margolis, B.L., Kroes, W.H. and Quinn, R.P. (1974) Job stress: an unlisted occupational hazard, *Journal of Occupational Medicine*, 16: 652–61.

Marmot, M.G., Rose, G., Shipley, M. and Hamilton, P.J.S. (1978) Employment grade and coronary heart disease in British civil servants, *Journal of Epidemiology and Community Health*, 32: 244–9.

Maslach, C. and Jackson, S.E. (1984) Burnout in organisational settings, *Applied Social Psychology Annual*, 5: 133–53.

Maslach, C. and Leiter, M. (1997) *The Truth About Burnout: How Organizations Cause Personal Stress and What to Do About it*. San Francisco, CA: Jossey-Bass.

Matthews, P. (1999) Stress in the workplace: The legal implications. http://www.stress.org.uk/stressin.htm

Medd, G. (1991) Stress Counselling in the Public Service, *Occupational Health Review*, June/July: 5–8.

Melandez, W.A. and Guzman, R.M. (1983) Burnout: The new academic disease, in Ashe-Eric, *Higher Education Research Report*, vol. 9. Washington DC: Association for the Study of HE.

Melhuish, A. (1993) Executive health, in D. Lock (ed.) *The Gower Handbook of Management*. Aldershot: Gower Publishing Ltd.

Mellott, R. (1992) *Stress Management for Professionals*. Boulder, CA: Career Track.

Mind Tools (1996) http://www.psychwww.com/mtsite/index.html

Miles, R.H. and Perreault, W.D. (1976) Organisational Role Conflict: Its Anteced-
ents and Consequences, *Organisational Behaviour and Human Performance*,
17: 19–44.

Miller, S. (1999) Council pays £67,000 for stress injury, *The Guardian*, 6 July.

Mitchell, R.E., Cronkite, R.C. and Moos, R.H. (1983) Stress, coping and
depression among married couples, *Journal of Abnormal Psychology*, 92(4):
433–48.

Newton, T. with Handy, J. and Fineman, S. (1995) *Managing Stress: Emotion
and Power at Work*. London: Sage.

O'Leary, L. (1990) Stress, emotion and human immune function, *Psychological
Bulletin*, 108: 363–82.

Palmer, C. (1994) Pressure mounts on stress, *Observer*, 10 July.

Powell, T. (1992) *The Mental Health Handbook*. Bicester: Winslow Press.

Pritchett, P. and Pound, R. (1997) *A Survival Guide to the Stress of Organisational
Change*. Dallas, TX: Pritchett & Associates.

Quick, J.C., Murphy, L.R. and Hurrell, J.J. (eds) (1992) *Stress and Well Being at
Work: Assessments and Interventions for Occupational Mental Health*. Washington, DC: American Psychological Association.

Rice, P.L. (1992) *Stress and Health*. Pacific Grove, CA: Brookes/Cole.

Robertson, I.T. (1983) *Human Behaviour in Organisations*. Plymouth: MacDonald
& Evans.

Rosenbaum, M. (1989) Self-control under stress: the role of learned resource-
fulness, *Advances in Behaviour Research & Therapy*, 11(4): 249–58.

Rosenham, D.L. and Seligman, M.E.P. (1989) *Abnormal Psychology*. New York:
Norton.

Royal College of Nursing (1992) *The Costs of Stress and the Costs and Benefits
of Stress Management*. London: RCN.

Selye, H. (1950) *Stress*. Montreal: Acta.

Selye, H. (1956) *The Stress of Life*. New York: McGraw-Hill.

Selye, H. (1974) *Stress Without Distress*. Philadelphia, CA: Lippincott.

Snape, J. (1988) Stress factors among lecturers in a college of further education,
Work & Stress, 1(4): 327–31.

Sparrow, A. (1998) Bosses could face court for stressing out their workers,
Daily Mail, 1 September.

Stephens, G.L. (1980) *Pathophysiology for Health Practitioners*. New York:
MacMillan.

Stewart, W. (1998) *Building Self-esteem: How to Replace Self-doubt with Confidence
and Well-being*. Oxford: How To Books.

Stress Management Research Associates (1998) Perspectives on coping.
http://www.stresscontrol.com/

Sussman, B. (1999) How to overcome stress, anxiety, depression and more in
the comfort of your own home. http://www.expert.help.com/anxiety

Sutton, J. (1998) *Thriving on Stress*. Plymouth: Plymbridge House.

Theorell, T. (1989) Personal control about work and health: a review of
epidemiological studies in Sweden, in A. Steptoe and A. Appels (eds) *Stress,
Personal Control and Health*. Chichester: John Wiley.

Tivey, H. (1979) *RSI Hazards Handbook: A Worker's Guide to Repetitive Strain
Injuries and How to Prevent Them*. London: Hazards Care Trust.

Townend, A. (1991) *Developing Assertiveness*. London: Routledge.

TUC (Trades Union Congress) (1996) *Survey of Safety Reps*. London: TUC.

Universities and Colleges Employers Association (1999) *Dealing with Stress in Higher Education: How to Get Started*. London: UCEA.

Walker v Northumberland County Council [1995] 1 RLR 35.

Wardell, W.I., Hyman, M. and Bahnson, C.B. (1964) Stress and coronary heart disease in three field studies, *Journal of Chronic Diseases*, 17: 73–84.

Weaver, M. (1999) Official who couldn't face the public wins £67,000, *Daily Telegraph*, 6 July.

Wilkinson, G. (1997) *Understanding Stress*. Banbury, Oxon: Family Doctor Publications in association with BMA.

Wilson, E. (1998) £239m bill to stop Britons feeling so depressed, *Daily Mail*, 10 September.

Wilson, P. (1993) Review of Personality and Stress – Individual Differences in the Stress Process, WorkSafe Western Australia (WWA) (1999). http://www1.safetyline.wa.gor.au/pagebin/wswagen10035.htm. *British Journal of Psychology*, 84(4): 557.

Yerkes, R.M. and Dodson, J.D. (1908) The relation of strength of stimulus to rapidity of habit-formation. *Journal of Comparative and Neurological Psychology*, 18: 459–82.

INDEX